# A Checklist for Preparing the Research Paper

|  | Date Due | Date Completed |
|---|---|---|

**Topic**
- ☐ Does the subject meet the criteria of the assignment?
- ☐ Has the subject been approved by the instructor?

**Outline**
- ☐ Has the thesis statement been written?
- ☐ Is the outline form correct?
- ☐ Does every item in the outline relate directly to the thesis statement?

**Text**
- ☐ Does everything in the paper show a direct relation to the subject?
- ☐ Is the paper well organized?
- ☐ Is the grammar (sentence structure, spelling, punctuation, and so on) correct?
- ☐ Is every quotation essential to the text?
- ☐ Are all quotations accurate?
- ☐ Are quotations integrated with the text?

**Documentation**
- ☐ Are all sources of information made clear to the reader?
- ☐ Are footnotes in the proper form?
- ☐ Are all footnotes coordinated numerically with the text?

**Bibliography**
- ☐ Have enough sources of information been used?
- ☐ Have scholarly materials been used?
- ☐ Are both books and periodicals represented?
- ☐ Is bibliographic form correct?
- ☐ Is the form of annotation correct?

**Presentation Form**
- ☐ Is the title page complete?
- ☐ Has the paper been given a final proofreading, to guard against typographical errors?
- ☐ Are all illustrations, graphs, charts, and so on labeled?
- ☐ Are all quotations typed in the proper forms?
- ☐ Are all the pages securely fastened together?

# The Research Paper Form and Content

## Third Edition

## Audrey J. Roth

**Wadsworth Publishing Company, Inc.**
**Belmont, California**

English Editor: Randy Cade
Production Editor: Connie Martin
Designer: Nancy Benedict
Copy Editor: Carol Dondrea
Cover Photograph: James Griffin

Printed in the United States of America
1 2 3 4 5 6 7 8 9 10—82 81 80 79 78

**Library of Congress Cataloging in Publication Data**

Roth, Audrey J.
  The research paper.

  Includes bibliographical references and index.
  1. Report writing.   I. Title.

LB2369.R66   1978   808'.023   77-13322
ISBN 0-534-00574-8

# Contents

## 1

## Starting the Research Paper     3

**Five Steps to a Research Paper**     **5**
Step 1. Choosing the Topic          5
Step 2. Collecting Information       5
Step 3. Evaluating Materials         6
Step 4. Organizing Ideas             6
Step 5. Writing the Paper            6

**What a Research Paper *Is***     **7**

**What a Research Paper *Is Not***     **8**

**Why a Research Paper Is Important**     **9**

## 2

## Choosing a General Topic     11

**Assigned Topics**     **11**

**Field-of-Study Topics**     **12**
Printed Aids          13
Your Own Interests    19

**Free-Choice Topics**     **22**

**Topics to Avoid**     **26**

# 3

## Narrowing the Topic    29

**Focusing on a Subject for**
**Research**                                   **31**
Subdividing                                    31
Free Association                               32
The Five Ws                                    33

**Finding an Approach**                        **35**
Examining                                      36
Comparing and Contrasting                      37
Relating                                       37
Arguing                                        38

## Collecting Information    39

**Primary and Secondary Sources**             **39**
**Where to Find Information**                  **40**
The Card Catalog                               41
Author Card                                    42
Title Card                                     42
Subject Card                                   43
"See also" Cards                               44
Catalog Customs                                44
Periodical Indexes                             46
Magazine Indexes                               46
Newspaper Indexes                              48
Using Periodical Indexes                       48
Bibliographies                                 49
Additional Sources of Information              50
More Library Sources                           51
Sources Outside the Library                    52

**The Preliminary Bibliography**              **53**
Uses of the Preliminary
Bibliography                                   54
Preliminary Bibliography Forms                 54

# 5

## Recording Information    58

**Evaluating Source Materials**          **58**

**Taking Notes**                         **60**
    Direct Quotation                61
    Summary                         62
    Paraphrase                      63
    Combination                     64
    Personal Comments, Ideas,
       Opinions                    65
    Unconscious Plagiarism          66

**Qualities of Good Notes**              **67**
    Legibility                      67
    Accuracy                        69
    Completeness                    72

**A Note about Photocopying**            **73**

**Number of Notecards**                  **74**

**Reference Words and
  Abbreviations**                **74**

# 6

## Organizing Ideas    76

**The Thesis Statement**                 **78**

**What a Thesis Statement Is *Not***     **79**

**Methods of Organizing Content**        **81**
    Time                            82
    Known to Unknown or
       Simple to Complex           82
    Comparison and Contrast         82
    General to Particular or
       Particular to General       83
    Problem to Solution or
       Question to Answer          83
    Cause to Effect or Effect to Cause   83

**Outlines**                             **84**
    Outline Form                    85

Outline Contents 87

**Revising Outlines** 90

# (7)

## Writing the Paper  92

**Writing Style** 92

**Good Openings** 93

**Bad Openings** 97

**Writing the Body of the Paper** 97
Unity 98
Coherence 98
Emphasis 99
Consistency 99
Clarity 99
Conciseness 100
Concreteness 100

**Good Endings** 100

**Bad Endings** 102

**Revising the Paper** 103
Word Choice and
    Sentence Structure 103
Mechanics 104
Smooth Transitions 104
Accuracy 104
Quality of Writing 105

**Selecting a Title** 105

# 8

## Documentation  107

**Direct Quotations** 107
Prose Quotations 108
Poetry Quotations 109
Dramatic Quotations 110

**Punctuating Quotations** 110

**Introducing Quoted Material**    **111**

**Maps, Charts, Diagrams, Pictures**    **112**

**Borrowed Ideas**    **112**

**Location of Documentation**    **113**
Endnotes    113
Footnotes    114
Interlinear Notes    114
In-Text Documentation    115

**Content of Notes**    **116**

**Writing the Notes**    **117**

**Numbering System**    **117**

**Form of Documentation Notes**    **118**
First References    118
Subsequent References    119

**Special Problems in
  Documentation**    **121**
One Author Quoted By Another    121
Casebooks and Sourcebooks    121
Readers    122
Plays    123
Biblical Quotations    123
Nonprint Media    124

**Forms for Natural and
  Social Sciences**    **124**

# 9

## Final Presentation    126

**Typing**    **127**

**Proofreading**    **127**

**Title Page**    **128**

**Outline**    **128**

**The Text**    **129**

**Notes**    **129**

**Illustrative Materials**    **130**

**Bibliography**      **130**

**Annotation**      **132**

**Preface**      **133**

**Synopsis or Abstract**      **133**

**Appendix**      **134**

# Appendix A
## A Selected List of Reference Works Available in Libraries   135

**General Reference Works**      **136**

  General      136

  Atlases      136

  Biography      136

  Dictionaries      137

  Encyclopedias      137

  Periodical Indexes      138

**Natural Sciences**      **138**

  General      138

  Agriculture      138

  Applied Science      139

  Biology      139

  Chemistry      139

  Geology      139

  Physics and Mathematics      140

**Social Sciences**      **140**

  General      140

  Business      140

  Economics      141

  Education      141

  Geography      141

  History      141

  Political Science      141

  Psychology      142

  Sociology      142

**Humanities**      **142**

  Art and Architecture      142

  Literature      143

Music and Dance                    144
Philosophy and Religion            144

# Appendix B
## Bibliography and Documentation Forms    146

**Conventions**                              **146**

**Bibliography**                             **147**

**Standard Forms for Bibliography**          **148**
Books                                148
Periodicals                          153
Other Sources                        154

**Documentation**                            **158**

**Standard Forms for Notes**                 **158**
Books                                158
Periodicals                          163
Other Sources                        165

# Appendix C
## Student Research Paper

"Roslyn: Evolution of a Literary
Character" by Judith Matz      169

# Preface

Sometimes formal education—the classroom—encourages passivity. Students feel anonymous: just another name on the roll sheet, another student number. They listen to lectures, are on the fringes of class discussions, watch films. The material may be too hard or too easy, or just too boring. It is an impersonal way of learning—if, indeed, any learning is going on—and "tuning out" is easy and inviting. Good test-takers find it easy to get by; many feel that school has little to offer them.

Students and teachers agree that some of the most exciting—and personal—education is active: the accidental discovery, the sudden insight, the fitting together of pieces of information, the working out of a problem. These are the personal encounters, the "payoff" in education, the kind of learning that classrooms can direct people to and encourage them in—but cannot provide. This learning comes from classroom stimulation, but most often takes place when a student is alone with books and notes and thoughts.

The research paper, assigned in a classroom and perhaps checked at various stages by an instructor, involves the student in an ideal, individual, and active learning process. It is a structure within which students can make the exciting discoveries of knowledge and of self that are basic to education. The research paper presents a chance for every student to exhibit individuality. And to produce a good research paper is a thoroughly satisfying experience!

Yet, most students approach the task with trepidation. Fulfilling the assignment is viewed as overcoming an obstacle rather than as accomplishing a goal. Sometimes the thought of having to write a number of pages is most disconcerting ("I know I could *tell* you about it!"). Often, the very idea of having to work independently baffles ("How should I *start?*").

This book doesn't guarantee to rid anyone of genuine concerns or to provide a magic formula that makes everything easy. It *does*, however, offer a procedure to follow and a framework to use in preparing a research paper. It has been used successfully by students and improved, in this third edition, by their comments and those of their teachers. As a result, many questions often asked by students have been anticipated and answered in the text. The book is meant to be a guide from the very beginning of the research process (choosing a topic) to the submission of a written paper in standard form. The book is also helpful if the researched material is presented orally, as a film or on slides and tape, or in some combination of media.

The emphasis in *The Research Paper* is on *ideas*—on how students can make researching meaningful and useful. Mostly, it suggests how people can work on their own. Chapter 1 is an overview of the research paper and the process of producing one. Since selecting a topic suitable for research is of prime importance, Chapters 2 and 3 are devoted to this aspect of the work; attention to them will prevent false starts and vague topics. Chapter 4, about collecting information, is a guide to the library and other sources of material (Appendix A gives additional suggestions), and Chapter 5 shows how to take notes (and avoid plagiarism) that lead to good writing. Emphases in Chapters 6 and 7 are on possible ways of organizing and writing the research paper. The conventions of documentation, explained in Chapter 8 (and, additionally, in Appendix B), follow the guidelines given in the *MLA Handbook for Writers of Research Papers, Theses, and Dissertations* (1977), and acknowledgment is made of variations commonly used in the social sciences and natural sciences. The book, therefore, is useful for many kinds of courses. Matters of presentation are the subject of Chapter 9.

Many examples of the steps in this research and writing process are taken from the sample research paper by a student in Appendix C, a paper students may use as a guide to their own writing. Other examples are from technical and vocational studies and the natural sciences, as well as from the humanities and social sciences. Throughout, I have attempted to show that the research paper is a flexible form within which students and teachers may work.

Finally, in this third edition, I have again tried to present a completely useful text with information relevant to the sorts of research paper assignments students are likely to receive today. My purpose, as in earlier editions, is to help students feel that a research paper is not an impossibly formidable assignment but, rather, one that can bring satisfaction and success.

Many students, of course, have contributed to this book and I am grateful to all of them. Most particularly, I am indebted to those who permitted me to include their work. The staff members at Miami-Dade Community College libraries, both North and South, who assisted me at various times were always pleasant and helpful. Finally, my thanks go to those colleagues whose comments have helped to make this revision an even more useful book for students: Andrew Halford, Paducah Community College (Kentucky); Janet Hennis, Citrus College; S. Clark Hulse, University of Illinois Chicago Circle; William Jameson, Brevard Community College; and Ralph Wirfs, Clatsop Community College (Oregon).

As always, this book is for my family—and now, also, for its two new members.

# The Research Paper

# 1
## Starting the Research Paper

The word *research* may conjure up any number of pictures. Perhaps it is that of a white-coated laboratory scientist working amid chemical containers and intricate glass tubing. Or it may be that of a bespectacled scholar reading musty volumes in a dimly lit alcove of a library. Or perhaps it is of a modishly dressed interviewer stopping people in a shopping center to ask about their choice of toothpaste.

Actually, each picture illustrates research, for although each activity is different, they all represent careful, serious, and systematic investigations.

*Research* means "to seek out again," and although much research is a matter of seeking out ideas and materials discovered by others in order to put them together in new ways, some research is aimed at finding what has never before been known.

*Pure research* may be carried on by a scientist in a laboratory—or by a landing vehicle scooping up surface samples on Mars or by people feeding into computers the radio signals sent here from that planet. This sort of research, usually associated with the natural sciences, aims at adding new knowledge to the totality of what people have been able to learn, even if such knowledge has no immediate or practical use beyond the knowing itself.

*Scholarly research* is similar to pure research except that the searcher works mainly through written records rather than with the materials of the physical world. This kind of research fits the most literal definition of the word (that is, "to find again"). Students do scholarly research when they prepare research papers for courses; their teachers do it when they write papers for journals and speeches for professional organizations.

*Applied research* attempts to make practical application of what has already been discovered or what has been theorized. Once nylon was developed, for instance, scientists in applied research found ways to use it in such diverse products as hosiery, carpets, and fishing line.

One form of applied research is *technical* or *business research.* A business person who must make practical decisions—choosing the location of a new manufacturing plant, for example—relies on this kind of research. Studies on natural resource availability, transportation access, financing, population, local employment, and educational availability—all part of such research—may be done before a final decision is reached.

*Market research,* the study of what consumers want, has resulted in uncounted new and different goods and services. Roll-out refrigerators, snowmobiles, nonstick zippers, and dog-walking services are among the many developed because research showed there were customers for each.

Although the purposes of these different kinds of research vary, the method of each is essentially the same: facts are gathered and interpreted so that conclusions can be drawn.

Students are asked to do research of one or more of these kinds. The assignment may be called a "term paper," a "library report," an "investigative report," or a "research paper"—the names are often used interchangeably. Whatever the name, the assignment will require that you locate information on a given subject (generally, but not always or exclusively, in a library) and write down conclusions based on your findings.

Perhaps in elementary or high school you did some "library work" on a subject: recorded the facts you discovered and handed in the result. That was a *report.* Typical subjects might be events in the life of William Faulkner, the battles of Alexander the Great, requirements for membership in a particular union, a résumé of the plot of *The Cheyenne Social Club,* or an explanation of how fish breathe. Reports simply convey information gathered or record a series of facts—often from a single source. No evaluation or interpretation, none of your own ideas, is required in a report.

A *research paper* differs from a simple report in one major way: *you* must be a participant in what you write. Preparing a research paper requires that you develop a point of view toward your material, take a stand, express some original thought. It is not enough simply to record the ideas of other people when you write a research paper—though of course you will want to be familiar with the ideas of others on the subject of your study. But in addition to gathering facts and ideas, you must interpret, analyze, evaluate, and draw conclusions from them.

Length has nothing to do with whether the finished work is a report or a research paper—content makes the difference. Sometimes length is specified in advance; sometimes it is determined by the complexity of the material (and sometimes by a student's willingness to work). In this book, we shall assume that a research paper runs from 1,500 to 3,000 words, or from six to twelve typewritten pages—standard length for most college-level work.

Research papers are as likely to be assigned in nursing, forestry management, and accounting as in English, history, anthropology, or chemistry. Indeed, research may be undertaken in any field. Whatever the school course or the subject of the paper, your goals will be the same: to learn from a study you undertake, to present your material competently, and to earn as high a grade (or as much satisfaction) as possible. You can achieve these goals most readily if you follow an orderly procedure from the time the paper is assigned until you turn it in. Instead of looking for shortcuts, concentrate on doing each of the following steps carefully and completely. If some parts of the process seem tedious at first, don't worry—you'll find them easier as they become more familiar. And if some of the instructions that follow sound unnecessary, remember that many people have found them the best of several possibilities.

The completed research paper, whatever its length and whatever its subject, will be the result of your having taken only five steps.

## Five Steps to a Research Paper

### Step 1. Choosing the Topic

Choosing the right topic has resulted in more good papers than probably any other single element in preparing a research paper. This first step is basic to everything else you do—so basic that Chapters 2 and 3 are devoted to helping you with the task.

If you are to choose your own topic rather than select one from a prepared list, remember that specific topics make better papers than very broad or generalized ones. "International Cooperation as Exemplified by the World Bank," "The Use of Laser Beams in Eye Surgery," or "Aristotle's Theory of Tragedy and *High Noon*" are bound to result in better research papers than such general topics as "The Importance of Economics," "Surgery," and "Philosophers and Their Philosophies."

### Step 2. Collecting Information

Choosing a topic for research, Step 1, is something you may do mostly at your desk. For this second step, however, you will probably go to the library and take notes on your studies there. Or, you may have to go outside the library—for instance, to interview the corner shoemaker or the chief chemist of an aluminum anodizing plant, to examine a proposed building site, or to follow the ecological effects of cleaning a pond.

It is possible that you already have some knowledge of your chosen subject to incorporate into your paper, but most of what you eventually write about will have to be sought out. In this second step you will be largely concerned with the *search* in "research."

### Step 3. Evaluating Materials

A good research paper reflects a critical attitude toward the facts collected and gives evidence of original thinking. Although these qualities must underlie all your work, you will be particularly aware of them during this third step as you begin to study the material you have gathered and develop a point of view toward it. You may decide to omit certain aspects of the topic previously thought important or to examine additional aspects.

By the time you have finished evaluating the information collected, your own ideas about your investigation will be almost completely formulated. At this point, you will also have had time to develop an attitude toward your material and take a stand—the requisites for a research paper.

### Step 4. Organizing Ideas

A collection of musical notes can be either random noise or a melody. A collection of nuts, bolts, and rods can be a scrap-metal pile or a useful machine. The results in each case depend on how the materials at hand are put together.

In the same way, a collection of facts, quotations, and ideas can be either meaningless or purposeful. If the materials are well organized—coordinated and arranged to lead logically to a conclusion—they can become a successful research paper. Therefore, putting notes together before you begin writing the paper is crucial. Chapter 6 will help you organize material before you begin to write.

### Step 5. Writing the Paper

If all the preparatory work of the previous four steps is carefully and thoughtfully completed, writing the paper is relatively easy. It is simply a matter of getting down on paper what you have learned and what you believe about the topic.

Allow enough time to make at least one revision before the final paper is due; most writers need several additional looks at what they have written to be sure they have said everything they want in the most effective way. Then, to complete the research paper, you need only add complete documentation and a bibliography, both in customary form, and make a final copy.

## What a Research Paper *Is*

When you have taken these five steps, you will have created something entirely new, a work that cannot be found anywhere else. If it is the kind of research paper being described in this book, it will have a number of qualities that reflect *you*, that make it your special creation. Such a research paper has the following characteristics:

(1)  *It synthesizes your discoveries about a topic and your evaluation of those discoveries.* The discoveries consist in large part of the ideas, knowledge, and actual words of experts in the field you have investigated. But all that would be valueless in a research paper unless you weighed the discoveries you made and drew conclusions from them. Notice that *you* are very much involved in this definition of what a research paper is, for it is writing that reflects your own ideas as much as those of anyone else who has written on the subject. Selecting information to use is a personal process; deciding how to approach this information, developing a point of view toward it, and, finally, choosing your own words to present it, are all highly personal activities.

(2)  *It is a work that shows your originality.* The paper resulting from your studies, evaluation, and synthesis will be a totally new creation, something that has originated with you. True, you will have put many hours of thought and much effort into a research paper that takes only a short time to read. But it is a real art to make the difficult appear easy, not to let an audience be aware of preparation and practice. Those papers that read most easily are often the result of the most work —and the fact that you have created an original paper will show.

(3)  *It acknowledges all sources that have been used.* Though your research paper is a new and original work, you will have consulted a number of sources in preparing it, and you will certainly want to acknowledge those sources. There are several ways a writer can provide documentation and acknowledgment in the research paper; these will

be discussed in Chapter 8. (Detailed examples of most traditional forms appear in Appendix B.)

## What a Research Paper *Is Not*

If you accept the definition just offered—that a research paper is a synthesis of your ideas and the material supplied to you by others, that it is original, and that it documents source material—you will never make the mistake of attempting to hand in what is certainly *not* a research paper.

(1) *A summary of an article or a book is not a research paper.* A single source does not permit you to be selective of materials and does not lead you to exercise judgment. Furthermore, since summaries usually follow the order of the original contents, not even the organization can be your own. Summaries of written (or visual or audible) materials have their uses, but substituting for a research paper is not one of them.

(2) *The ideas of others, repeated uncritically, do not make a research paper.* If you are satisfied simply to repeat the conclusions of other people without weighing them against what you have learned, you will perhaps end up producing a satisfactory "report" of those findings, but you will not have done the kind of research paper this book is about. A biography of someone you do not know falls into this category of "report," unless you have been able to discover new information about the person or otherwise include your own ideas. Furthermore, if you merely repeat the conclusions of other people without even bothering to investigate what they are talking about, you will not have a research paper. For example, no amount of reading *about* a novel or poem can substitute for reading the work itself, any more than reading about a musical group can substitute for hearing the people play.

(3) *A series of quotations, no matter how skillfully put together, does not make a research paper.* Quotations have an important place in a paper; they are the words of experts in the field and can support your own ideas. But if your paper consists of quotations alone, the "you" of the synthesis is missing; you yourself are not involved in such a paper, and the paper does not evidence any originality. Furthermore, you will find it difficult to organize dozens of quotations into a coherent whole with logical transitions, and the work cannot have a consistent style since it is made of the words of many writers. If the quotations come from a variety of sources, it is all but impossible to make them into anything more than a patchwork. If they come from a single source, they will certainly lack the originality required of a research paper.

(4)  *Unsubstantiated personal opinion does not constitute a research paper.* If you have truly done research for an assignment, you will have discovered information on which to base your own ideas. And in order for someone to decide if your conclusions are valid, you will need to present the facts that lead to your conclusions as well as the conclusions themselves.

Suppose you express the opinion that schools can operate very well without administrators and that therefore administrators should be done away with immediately. This is an unusual idea, and anyone reading your words would be justifiably suspicious of the statement. However, if you can cite experiments conducted by schools X, Y, and Z indicating that students learned more quickly and that operations went smoothly without administrators in the buildings, you will have supported with evidence what is otherwise only personal opinion.

(5)  *Copying or accepting another person's work without acknowledging it, whether the work is published or unpublished, professional or amateur, is not research; it is plagiarism.* It is morally wrong to pass off as your own any writing you did not do, or to present such work without acknowledgment of a source and therefore allow someone to assume it is yours. Accepting and turning in a research paper done by another student or purchased from a supplier of such papers is indefensible. There are laws against plagiarism, and in many schools any student involved in plagiarism is automatically dismissed.

On the most literal level, perhaps no word or thought is completely original; you must have learned it somewhere. Often only the finest line of distinction separates what must be credited in a research paper from what you can safely present as original. What requires credit to avoid plagiarism and what does not is discussed in Chapters 5 and 8. Suffice it to say now that students who respect themselves and their work will not be tempted to copy from anyone and will always extend proper credit for ideas, as well as for specific wording.

## Why a Research Paper Is Important

Since the research paper involves your ability to gather information, examine it critically, think creatively, organize effectively, and write convincingly, it is a project that allows you to demonstrate a great many skills that are as basic to business and professional life as they are to academic success. Business people employ these same research processes when deciding whether to switch to a new model for the company airplane, to stop manufacturing a product, or to promote a worker. Lawyers daily use the method of finding, analyzing, and organizing facts, whether they are preparing a murder case for courtroom presentation or incorporating a new business. Journalists use these skills every time they write a story; politicians use them in every speech. Physicians need to find, analyze, and organize facts for presentation when they make a diagnosis. So do air conditioning specialists, flight engineers, fashion designers, and many others in their everyday work.

In short, teachers do not assign research papers capriciously. Several reasons, in addition to the sharpening of the skills noted, commend the research paper as a popular and valuable assignment.

One is that many kinds of writing—essay tests, for instance—require students to gather and process factual information on specific subjects just as a research paper does. Newspapers and magazine articles—even books—are the result of the same skills, and though one might never become a published writer, one becomes a more perceptive reader for knowing about the writing processes.

There is an enormous sense of achievement in working independently to fulfill a goal—as one must in completing a research paper. Also, there is satisfaction in having written something good, of having done a job to the best of your ability, and of knowing that you are an "expert" on a subject. Not the least of these personal satisfactions, of course, is having your efforts rewarded by a high grade on the assignment.

But there are still other reasons why a research paper can be important to you. It offers you the chance to investigate something you may have wanted to know about. Or to find out about a subject you think you may be interested in, but cannot take a course in at the moment.

And if you have ever chafed at not being able to express your own ideas or attain recognition in a large student body, the research paper can become an ideal vehicle, for if it truly reflects you and your thinking; it will also establish you as an individual. When reading it, your instructor is concentrating only on you and your work. And since it is entirely your own, you can use the paper to express your own ideas and demonstrate your own capabilities.

Finally, you show your ability to weigh words, discriminate among ideas, and draw conclusions when you prepare a research paper. In other words, this project calls upon you to exercise that form of judgment called *critical thinking*. Of all that you have to gain from education, probably the most desirable gain is this one: the habit of thinking critically.

# 2

# Choosing a General Topic

Research papers are usually assigned at the beginning of a term and are due shortly before the term ends. Therefore, you have plenty of time to gather information, mull over ideas, write your paper, and revise it several times before turning it in. If you decide early in the term on a general area or topic for study, you will have plenty of time to narrow the topic down, do research, and write the paper.

There are three kinds of research topics: *Assigned Topics,* selected by an instructor and presented to you (often the actual writing subject is given, too) ; *Field-of-Study Topics,* decided upon by you, but they must be related to the course in which the paper is assigned; and *Free-Choice Topics,* in which you are encouraged to investigate any area you choose. All research writing begins with these broad topics, though sometimes it seems that the choice of specific subject for writing (achieved by narrowing, as noted in Chapter 3) is telescoped with the topic selection so that the two separate processes seem as one.

## Assigned Topics

The teacher who assigns you a topic (or writing subject) or gives you a list of approved ones to choose from, is relieving you of one task in the preparation of the research paper. Such assignment is also giving you much help toward producing a successful research paper for, as you already know, a good topic is the beginning of a good paper. Vague, irrelevant, unwieldy, or too-narrow topics have little chance of achieving the focus and direction that make for a successful piece of writing.

Most of what are usually called "Assigned Topics" are actually *subjects,* already narrowed and ready for investigation: "Biblical Symbolism in *The Grapes of Wrath*," "Benjamin Franklin and the *Saturday Evening Post*," "The Mathematical Contributions of Leibniz."

Sometimes Assigned Topics are presented and you need to choose a specific subject for research. "Write on a subject related to a novel we will read this term" is a topic that allows for considerable variety in narrowing. For instance, if a novel to be read is *Being There* by Jerzy Kosinski, you might choose to relate it to one or more other novels by Kosinski, to compare it to Kosinski's beliefs about the place of television in individual development, to show how it is a book in the picaresque style, or to cite its possible origins in *Candide* and *The Republic*—all after reading the novel itself, of course. A biography of Kosinski would not be a particularly wise choice for a research paper although if you were able to find and concentrate on personal elements the author drew upon in developing *Being There,* you would be fulfilling the topic assigned.

An Assigned Topic provides you with many opportunities for personal expression in your research paper, for remember that this project depends heavily on what *you* have discovered and what *you* have to say on a subject.

## Field-of-Study Topics

Field-of-Study Topics are similar to the generalized form of Assigned Topic just discussed; however, you need to select the general area of study yourself. In order to do that, you will want to know something about the subject matter of the course for which you will write the research paper.

You can choose a topic early in the term if you have some knowledge of the course material from talking with friends, from having taken a prerequisite course, or from what the instructor tells you about the course. If you delay starting your paper until a week or so before it's due, you will probably know enough about the course to choose a related topic; but you may not have left yourself enough time to do a very good job on the research paper.

If you are conscientious and want to begin work soon after the assignment is given, or if you have to submit your topic for approval early in the course and you don't know enough about the course to make a good selection, you will find help in printed aids (your textbook, encyclopedias, library card catalogs, periodical indexes) and help through your own extracurricular interests.

## Printed Aids

Begin looking for a Field-of-Study Topic in your **textbook.** The table of contents alone will tell you a great deal about the course you are enrolled in and thus will help you decide on a research topic. If your book also contains an index or a glossary, read it too, in order to learn more about the contents.

For example, suppose your textbook is *Personality, Effective and Ineffective.*[1] The table of contents of this book shows that it contains eleven chapters: Studying Personality; Principles of Learning; Organic Influences on Personality; Motivation and Thinking; Social Learning and Personality; Conflict, Stress, and Neurosis; Effective Personality; Social Structure and Personality; Psychoanalysis: Theory and Therapy; Humanism: Theory and Therapy; Psychotherapy and Behavior Modification: Moving toward Eclecticism (see Figure 1).

You might begin by focusing on any one of these general topics, though the fact that they are chapters with subdivisions indicates that each is a fairly broad area of study. And you might have any sort of reason for choosing the particular topic: previous knowledge or interest, chance, having heard the words before. For example, Chapter 7 (Effective Personality) and the subdivision Personal Worth and Self-Esteem might suggest a study of how the emphasis on these factors is being used in elementary classrooms to encourage academically weak students or a study of what tests and test results on self-esteem indicate for therapists or one on how a sense of personal worth might be related to behavior modification. (A brief look at the contents of this section in the textbook might suggest other topics, too.)

This particular book has a name index (so do many other books), which lists people mentioned in the text; a study of the work or contributions of any of them could lead to a research paper subject. A glossary may serve the same purpose by providing important terms related to the subject of the book, thus presenting many key concepts of the course before they are studied individually.

If the preface or introduction of your textbook contains more than a summary of the contents, you may be able to choose a subject for research from the ideas in it. If the textbook is an anthology, the authors of the various contributions may be people whose work bears investigation for a Field-of-Study Topic.

So, ideas for research paper subjects can come from the table of contents, the indexes or glossaries, the preface or introduction, and from the contributors (if there are any) of your textbook.

An **encyclopedia** is another place to find ideas for a Field-of-Study research paper. The principal value of reading an encyclopedia article

[1] David G. Martin (Monterey: Brooks/Cole, 1976).

on the subject of a course (or on a related subject) is the overall view
it will give you.

    Suppose you need a research topic for a marine biology course. The
sea interests you, but obviously that's too much to write a classroom
paper about. Then you think of the tides in the ocean. The *Encyclopedia
Americana* (1975) entry about tides has a number of divisions, each with
subdivisions: Tidal Actions (which includes Kinds of Tides; Tidal

# *Contents*

## 1

### Studying Personality
#### 1

Defining Personality    1
Theories of Personality    3
The Nature of Evidence    4
Measuring Personality    11
The Personal Impact of Studying
    Personality    20
Summary    22

## 2

### Principles of Learning
#### 24

Classical Conditioning    24
Instrumental (Operant)
    Conditioning    33
Aversive Conditioning    40
Summary    51

## 3

### Organic Influences on Personality
#### 53

The Nervous System    54
Chemical Influences    75
Genetics and Personality    80
Summary    85

## 4

### Motivation and Thinking
#### 87

Motivation    87
Frustration and Conflict    106
Thinking    113
Summary    120

Current; Bore; Nontidal Phenomena), The Formation of Tides (including Tides and the Moon; Tidal Periods; Tides and the Sun; Earth and Atmospheric Tide), Development of Tidal Studies (containing Tidal Theory; The Harmonic Method; Establishment of Datum Planes), and Tidal Study Today (including Computer Techniques and Study of Worldwide Tidal Patterns). Any of these subjects would do for a Field-of-Study research paper.

# 5

**Social Learning and Personality**
122

Principles of Social Learning    123
Applying the Principles    137
Summary    154

# 6

**Conflict, Stress, and Neurosis**
156

External and Internal Cues in
    Conflict    157
An Apparent Neurotic Paradox    160
Anxiety-Avoiding Behaviors
    ("Symptoms")    165
Defense, Repression, and Unconscious
    Influences on Behavior    172
Anxiety States    182
Anxiety and Learning    184
Other Behavior Disorders    189
Summary    191

# 7

**Effective Personality**
193

Attempts to Describe the Effective
    Personality    194
An (Inevitably Biased) Attempt at
    Consensus    199
Personal Worth and Self-Esteem    202
Autonomy and Self-Control    206
Accurate, Full Experiencing    212
Relationships and Intimacy    215
Summary    220

# 8

**Social Structure and Personality**
222

Culture and Personality    223
Cultural Differences    225
The Mountain People    231
Social Status and Personality    235
Social Engineering    241
Summary    254

Fig. 1    Textbook table of contents, an aid to finding a Field-of-Study Topic. (From *Personality: Effective and Ineffective* by D. G. Martin. Copyright © 1976 by Wadsworth Publishing Company, Inc. Reprinted by permission of the publisher, Brooks/Cole Publishing Company, Monterey, California.)

Figure 2 reproduces the last page of this article. Many of the paragraphs suggest shorter research papers, and the paragraph about publications on tide might give you even other ideas.

Besides giving you a general view of a subject, an encyclopedia article offers you other aids to choosing a research topic. It often directs you to articles in the encyclopedia on related subjects. (The entry on deserts in the same encyclopedia directs the reader to articles on the Gobi and Sahara, as well as to those on the Antarctic and Arctic.)

The bibliography that concludes many encyclopedia articles directs you to books in the field; if you consult some of these books, you may find a research topic that seems interesting and appropriate.

The **card catalog** of a library is the third source you may consult to find a subject for research related to the course for which you must write the paper.[2] The catalog contains at least three card entries for each nonfiction book in the library: one filed by author, one by title, and one by subject.

Begin your search by consulting the cards filed under the subject heading. If you need to do research for an accounting course, look under "Accounting" in the card catalog. There you will find the names of books on accounting listed on individual cards.

Many general subjects also have "See also" cards filed in the catalog. "See also" cards refer you to related subject headings, where you can find more books to consult. For example, Figure 3 shows three cards listing subjects related to "Accounting." Under each of these headings, you will find cards for additional books you may examine as you have your textbook; you will discover that they, too, offer many topics for investigation.

Finally, study one of the **periodical indexes** for Field-of-Study research ideas. A specific index (*Education Index, Chemical Abstracts, Book Review Index,* and so on) will automatically put your search into the right area for the research you need to do. But a general index (for example, *New York Times Index, Readers' Guide to Periodical Literature*) will also yield topics you may draw from. And for both kinds of indexes you can apply the same method.

Suppose you must find a research paper topic for a social science survey course in which economics, psychology, anthropology, and sociology will be studied. You might look under one of those general headings. Or you might note in your textbook that there is mention of the role of women in relation to psychology and decide to look in the *Readers' Guide* under "Women" for some suggestions. Figure 4 reproduces a page from a *Readers' Guide* entry on that topic. Any of the subdivisions that appear under this entry (Employment, Occupations,

---

[2] Detailed information about the card catalog begins on page 41.

**Computer Techniques.** In the 1960's changes brought about by the development of electronic computers were made in all aspects of tidal observation, analysis, and prediction. Digital recorders have been installed on automatic tide gauges, providing sequential, point-to-point values of the height of a given tide. These data are routinely processed on computers to calculate the times and heights of high and low waters, mean ranges and inequalities, various tidal planes and monthly extremes, and the lunitidal intervals—the intervals between the moon's transit over the local or Greenwich meridian and the following high or low water.

New analysis procedures have been developed for obtaining the amplitude and phase lag for each constituent of the tide. For example, a "least square" procedure has been programmed for large computers. This procedure solves for all constituents simultaneously, in contrast to the traditional Fourier analysis for one constituent at a time, which eliminates the effects of the other constituents from each result. (See HARMONIC ANALYSIS.) The newer procedure has been found to fit the recorded data somewhat more accurately. In addition, unlike Fourier analysis, it does not require an unbroken sequence of data equally spaced in time.

Electronic computers permit the specification of any frequencies in the prediction process, whereas the mechanical tide-predicting machines were limited to a finite set of frequencies for which appropriate gears were included in the basic design. In both Britain and the United States, studies of the prediction of shallow-water tides by harmonic methods exploited this newly found flexibility, using about 115 tidal constituents to permit more accurate analysis and prediction.

Research studies have used long series of data, for example, a list of 500,000 hourly readings of tidal heights taken over a 50-year period, to establish values of the *continuum*—the "noise," or nonpredictable variations in sea level—as a function of frequency. Determination of these values establishes the limits that may be achieved by even the best predicting procedures. Studies of this kind are also impossible without the use of electronic computers.

In addition, geophysicists Walter Munk of the United States and David Cartwright of Britain developed a "response" method of tide prediction. Weights are computed for a set of time-variable spherical harmonics of the gravitational potential and of radiant flux on the earth's surface to obtain an optimum fit to an observed series of tide heights. For predictions at another time, the same set of weights are then applied to a time series for the gravitational and radiational potentials for the required times.

**Study of Worldwide Tidal Patterns.** There are ordinarily about 1,000 tide gauges operating around the world at any given time. But for describing global patterns of the tide they could hardly be more poorly distributed. Most of them are at the mouths of harbors and on rivers, places for which tide predictions are a practical necessity. However, because the coastal features may severely modify both the amplitude and the phase of the ocean tide, the harbor and river observations have very limited use in attempts to depict tidal phenomena in the oceans.

Nevertheless, men have attempted for more than a century to use these data, together with

data gathered around islands, in preparing cotidal charts and co-range charts of the world. A *cotidal chart* is a set of lines on a chart, each line joining all points at which high water occurs at the same time. Similarly, a *co-range chart* has lines passing through places of equal tidal range. These charts are used in describing only a single harmonic constituent of the tide, so that in theory a chart would be needed for each constituent. In practice, however, charts have been attempted only for the major constituents: the lunar semidaily, solar semidaily, lunar-solar daily, and lunar daily. The principal effort has been applied to lunar semidaily charts, and the preparation of cotidal charts has received more attention than co-range charts.

The most critical aspect of cotidal charts is the location of *amphidromic points*. These are no-tide points from which the radiating cotidal lines progress through all hours of the tidal cycle. Even if there are some islands near these points for which tidal data are available, the "noise" to "signal," or significant data, ratio is large, and hence the data are less reliable when the range of tide is small.

An international program for measuring the tide in deep ocean was initiated in the mid-1960's. Free-fall gauges have been developed that record on the ocean floor and then are recalled to the surface by means of signals. Other bottom-mounted gauges, connected by cables to ships or to the shore, have also produced valuable data. The program to obtain a grid of tide stations covering the world's oceans will take a long time, but the data will be extremely useful for comparison with theoretical numerical studies of the world distribution of tides.

Although tidal characteristics change from place to place, tides in the Atlantic Ocean are basically semidaily, whereas Pacific Ocean tides tend to be mixed. There is some evidence that the tidal range observed on the east coast of the United States varies directly with the width of the continental shelf. Florida is in a somewhat unique tidal situation, having a semidiurnal tide at Miami, a mixed tide at Key West, and a diurnal tide at Pensacola.

**Publications.** The U. S. Coast and Geodetic Survey publishes annual tide tables for the entire world, in four volumes. Each volume contains daily predictions for key places and tables of time and height differences for secondary sites. There are also two annual volumes of tidal current tables, primarily for places in North America. In addition the survey publishes tidal current charts for a number of major harbors and estuaries. Most of the other important nautical countries publish their own tide tables in various formats.

BERNARD D. ZETLER, *ESSA Atlantic Oceanographic and Meteorological Laboratories, Miami*

**Bibliography**

Defant, Albert, *Physical Oceanography,* vol. 2 (New York 1961).
Dietrich, Gunter, *General Oceanography: An Introduction* (New York 1963).
Doodson, Arthur T., and Warburg, H. D., *Admiralty Manual of Tides* (London 1941).
Dronkers, Jo J., *Tidal Computations in River and Coastal Waters* (Amsterdam, the Netherlands, 1964).
Macmillan, D. Henry, *Tides* (New York 1966).
Munk, Walter H., and Zetler, Bernard D., "Deep Sea Tides: A Program," *Science,* vol. 158, No. 3803, Nov. 17, 1967.
Schuremen, Paul, *Manual of Harmonic Analysis and Prediction of Tides,* Coast and Geodetic Survey Special Publication No. 98 (Washington 1940).

Fig. 2   Page from an encyclopedia, an aid to developing a Field-of-Study Topic. (From the *Encyclopedia Americana,* Vol. 26, 1975. Copyright © 1975 by Americana Corporation. Reprinted by permission of the publisher.)

```
        Accounting
             See also
    Accounting and price fluctuations
    Accounts current
    Accounts receivable
    Amortization
    Auditing
    Average of accounts
    Bookkeeping
    Business losses
    Business mathematics
    Card system in business
                         (Continued on next card)


                          ◯
```

```
        Accounting                    (Card 2)
             See also
    Cost accounting
    Depreciation
    Financial statements
    Fiscal year
    Income accounting
    Inventories
    Liquidation
    Machine accounting
    Municipal finance—Accounting
    Productivity accounting

                          ◯
```

Fig. 3  "See also" cards from a library card catalog, showing subject headings under which books relating to the main topic, "Accounting," may be found. Accounting card shown opposite.


Psychology, Famous Women, Women and Men, Women and the Church, Women Artists, and so on) might serve as a starting place for determining a research topic. (Other editions of the *Readers' Guide* might contain additional listings.) The "See also" listings suggest additional topics.

```
Accounting
        See also subdivision Accounting under names
of industries, professions, trades, etc., e.g.,
Dairying-Accounting; Corporations-Accounting
```

You could, for example, start with the Ordination of Women in various faiths or Married Women and changes in the economy during a particular time because of their employment or the Sex Role of Women. (Each of these general topics would, of course, need to be narrowed down to a workable subject, as would any other Field-of-Study Topic.)

### Your Own Interests

Another way to select a Field-of-Study Topic is to relate the course content to your own vocational or avocational interests. This method of selecting a subject for research is often the most satisfactory because it allows students to study topics they believe useful to them in some way.

Suppose you want college to prepare you for a career in business. Are you interested in a particular aspect of business—manufacturing, real estate, airport management? Head a sheet of paper with the name of the subject to which you must relate your interest and draw a vertical line down the middle of the page. On one side of the line, write your vocational interest; on the other side, make a list of words related to the course for which you are preparing the research paper. Use words from the table of contents of your textbook, words specifying categories within the course you are taking, or words derived from free association with the material in the course.

JUNE 25, 1976

WISCONSIN
  See also
  Agriculture—Wisconsin
WIT and humor. See Humor
WIVES
  See also
  Married women
WOLF hunting
  Fear and loathing in wolf country. J. G. Mitchell.
    il Audubon 78:20-39 My '76
WOLFBEIN, Seymour L.
  Real story behind the unemployment figures;
    interview. il por Nations Bus 64:24-6+ My '76
WOLFF, Anthony
  World progress report. See occasional issues of
    Saturday review
WOLMAN, William
  Economic diary. See occasional issues of Busi-
    ness week
WOLVES
  Fear and loathing in wolf country. J. G.
    Mitchell. il Audubon 78:20-39 My '76
WOMAN suffrage
        United States
  Feminists and other useful fanatics. G. Wills.
    il Harper 252:35-8+ Je '76
WOMEN
  See also
  Ordination of women
        Employment
  When sisterhood turns sour. J. Curtis. il por
    N Y Times Mag p 15-16 My 30 '76
    See also
  Married women—Employment
        Occupations
  See also
  Saleswomen
        Psychology
  Gifted girls 50 years later; ongoing psychological
    study conducted by Stanford university re-
    searchers. Intellect 104:553-4 My '76
        Iran
  Sisters of the princess. K. Boyle. Nation 222:
    261-2 Mr 6 '76
        United States
  Liberated women: how they're changing Ameri-
    can life; interviews. J. Huber; U. Bronfen-
    brenner. pors U.S. News 80:46-9 Je 7 '76
    See also
  Woman suffrage—United States
WOMEN, Famous
  How those energetic women get that way. D.
    Kaye. il Redbook 147:102-3+ Je '76
WOMEN, Jewish. See Jewish women
WOMEN and men
  See also
  Sex role
WOMEN and religion
  Feminism: a new reformation; ed by F. X.
    Murphy. H. Küng. N Y Times Mag p34-5 My
    23 '76
WOMEN and the church. See Women and religion
WOMEN artists
  Art; exhibition: 7 American women: the depres-
    sion decade. L. Alloway. Nation 222:220-1
    F 21 '76
  Pains and pleasures of rebirth: women's body
    art. L. R. Lippard. bibl il Art in Am 64:
    73-81 My '76
  Women's art in the '70s. L. Alloway. bibl il
    Art in Am 64:64-72 My '76
WOMEN athletes
  All-American sports guide. il Harp Baz 109:
    72-3 My '76
WOMEN automobile racing drivers
  See also
  Guthrie, J.
WOMEN executives
  Why bosses turn bitchy. R. M. Kanter. bibl
    il por Psychol Today 9:56-7+ My '76
WOMEN in art
  Pains and pleasures of rebirth: women's body
    art. L. R. Lippard. bibl il Art in Am 64:73-81
    My '76
WOMEN in politics
  Emerging woman. il Am Home 79:14-15+ Je '76
WOMEN in publishing
  Feminist publishing: an exploration. R. Fein-
    berg and S. Vaughn. il Lib J 101:1263-5 Je
    1 '76
WOMEN in sales. See Saleswomen
WOMEN medical students. See Medical students
WOMEN publishers. See Women in publishing
WOMENS clothing industry. See Clothing industry
WOMEN'S liberation movement
  When sisterhood turns sour. J. Curtis. il por
    N Y Times Mag p 15-16 My 30 '76
WOOD, Abigail
  Relating; questions and answers. See issues of
    Seventeen

WOOD, David L. and others
  Western pine beetle: specificity among anan-
    tiomers of male and female components of
    an attractant pheromone. bibl il Science 192:
    896-8 My 28 '76
WOOD, Natalie
  At home with Natalie Wood & Robert Wagner.
    il pors Good H 182:134-9 Je '76
WOOD, Ralph C.
  Solzhenitsyn as latter-day prophet. il Chr Cent
    93:480-3 My 19 '76
WOODCOCK, Leonard
  Platform to stand on; Democrats; excerpt from ,
    address, May 18 1976. Nation 222:657-8 My
    29 '76
WOODWARD Bob
  Richard Nixon's Final days. N. Cousins. Sat
    R 3:4 My 15 '76 •
  Woodward & Bernstein's long goodbye. M. Jane-
    way. il pors Atlantic 237:98-100 Je '76 •
  Writing hot history. M. Lerner. Sat R 3:16-19
    My 29 '76 •
WOODWORKING
  See also
  Joinery
        Projects
  See also
  Chests
WOOL dyeing. See Dyes and dyeing
WORDS
  See also
  Spelling
WORDS in art
  Words. O. K. Chatt. il Sch Arts 75:40-2 Je '76
WORK
  Plain talk about working. I. Ross. il Mech
    Illus 72:58+ My '76
    See also
  Labor and laboring classes
WORKING classes. See Labor and laboring
    classes
WORLD of Sid and Marty Krofft, Atlanta. See
    Amusement parks
WORLEY, James
  Altaration; poem. Chr Cent 93:483 My 19 '76
WORM runner's digest
  Worm-breeding with tongue in cheek. J. V.
    McConnell. il UNESCO Courier 29:12-15+ Ap
    '76
WORMS
  See also
  Flatworms
WORMS, intestinal and parasitic
  See also
  Roundworms
WRIGHT, Keith, and Alin, Roy
  (eds) Junior high/middle school workshop. See
    issues of English journal
WU, Chien-shiung
  State of US physics—1976: adaptation of ad-
    dress, February 3, 1976. bibl il Phys Today
    29:23-5+ Ap '76
WUORINEN, Charles
  Tashi: Wuorinen premiere. Hi Fi 26:MA28 Je
    '76 •
WYKES, Robert
  St Louis sym: Adequate earth. Hi Fi 26:MA29
    Je '76 •

X RAY astronomy
  Five satellites observe short, intense X-ray
    bursts. G. B. Lubkin. il Phys Today 29:
    17+ Ap '76
X RAY crystallography. See Crystallography—X
    ray studies

YACHTS
        Design
  Drawing board (cont of) Designs. E. Brewer.
    See issues of Motor boating & sailing
        Valuation
  IRS lowers the boom; yacht donations. S.
    Stapleton. Motor B & S 137:58+ Je '76
YACHTS and yachting
  See also
  Cruisers (pleasure boats)
YANOVSKY, Sarit
  Seventeen in Israel; interview. ed by W.
    Novak. Seventeen 35:56+ Je '76
YARD lighting. See Lighting, Outdoor
YARDS. See Home grounds
YAROWSKY, P. J. and Carpenter, D. O.
  Aspartate: distinct receptors on aplysia neurons.
    bibl il Science 192:807-9 My 21 '76
YATES, Brock
  Great Pan-American weed fleet. Motor B & S
    137:60-1+ Je '76

Fig. 4  Page from the *Readers' Guide to Periodical Literature* showing
the range of entries under a single topic heading. (Copyright © 1975, 1976
by The H. W. Wilson Company. Material reproduced by permission of the
publisher.)

*Literature* (course for which you will write the research paper)

| 1. authors | | |
|---|---|---|
| 2. novels | (categories | |
| 3. nonfiction | of literature | airplanes (special |
| 4. plays | arrived at by | interest) |
| 5. eras | free | |
| 6. poems | association) | |
| 7. countries | | |

By combining each word in the left column with the word on the right, you can arrive at related ideas that will serve as general topic choices for the research paper. For example, if you make a connection between authors of literature (that is, writers) and airplanes or flying, you could use as a general topic choice "Pilots who write." Then, you may know some pilots who are authors (or authors who are pilots) and do research on one or several such people.

Here are examples of how each of the seven ideas listed under "Literature" can be related to airplanes and yield research paper topics:

1. People who fly and also write (the Lindberghs, Amelia Earhart, Antoine de St. Exupéry, the astronauts).
2. Novels about flying, especially war novels.
3. Developments in the aviation industry or use of aircraft for specific purposes (war, spying, speed) reported in book form (for example, in biographies of pilots).
4. Plays (or movies) about flying.
5. Ideas about flight evident in the mythology of ancient cultures.
6. Poetry about flying, especially poetry stemming from war or written by pilots.
7. Stories, real or imaginary, of flying in various countries.

Sometimes the relationship between your interest and a course content is more difficult to make but is still possible—if you're willing to be imaginative in making the relationships. Someone with a special interest in real estate who has to write a research paper for a philosophy course might jot down the following list:

*Philosophy*

| metaphysics | |
|---|---|
| ethics | |
| logic | real estate |
| history | |
| famous philosophers | |

The history of philosophy has nothing to do with real estate and it would be stretching too far to try to relate famous philosophers or metaphysics to real estate. Logic, however, does offer a possible topic: "Logical and Emotional Arguments in Selling Real Estate." Ethics also can provide a kind of relationship: "Ethical-Practice Codes for Real Estate Brokers," for example.

It is worthwhile trying this method even though there are some circumstances under which it will not work. When it *does* work, it gives you a chance to choose a subject that combines your own interests with those of the teacher who will read your research paper.

## Free-Choice Topics

Instead of a research paper within a particular field of study, you may be asked to do one on a topic completely of your own choice. Suddenly all of human knowledge is open to you, and you must pinpoint something from this vast area.

You can use the printed aids already suggested—textbooks, encyclopedias, the card catalog, and periodical indexes; but to start looking through any of them without direction is unnecessarily time-consuming. Therefore, you will do better to choose one of these other methods of selecting your research paper topic.

(1)   *Choose a topic with which you are familiar and about which you want to know more.* You may have had a history course and learned something about the Mayans but would like to learn more. Or perhaps you have done some reading on your own about witchcraft but didn't find much about medieval beliefs on the topic. Any area about which you have some knowledge bears further study and thus offers possibilities for a Free-Choice research paper.

(2)   *Choose a topic you know nothing about but would like to investigate.* Names you may have encountered once and then passed over—a Lysenko or a Grimmelshausen—or unusual terms, such as *cybernetics,* offer possibilities for investigation. Search your memory; what you remember being interested in or temporarily "stopped" by may well become your research topic.

(3)   *Browse through the library to find a topic that looks interesting enough to investigate.* Because the library contains information on every topic, gathered into general areas, just looking through the major divisions of the cataloging system should suggest possibilities for research.

Library books are cataloged by either the Library of Congress system or the Dewey Decimal Classification system. Each offers you a way of looking at a huge number of resources in some organized fashion.

The **Library of Congress system** divides the fields of knowledge into twenty-one groups, each one identified by a letter of the alphabet (except the letters I, O, W, X, and Y).

A    General works and polygraphy
B    Philosophy and religion
C    History and auxiliary sciences
D    History and topography (except America)
E–F    America
G    Geography and anthropology
H    Social sciences
J    Political science
K    Law
L    Education
M    Music
N    Fine arts
P    Language and literature
Q    Science
R    Medicine
S    Agriculture and plant and animal industry
T    Technology
U    Military science
V    Naval science
Z    Bibliography and library science

Each of these classifications is subdivided by letters; still further divisions are identified by a numerical range (see Figure 5).

The **Dewey Decimal Classification,** a number system developed by Melvil Dewey, divides reference works into ten classes: one category of general knowledge and nine categories of special knowledge. Each class is identified by a three-digit numeral:

000–099 Generalities
100–199 Philosophy and related
200–299 Religion
300–399 The social sciences
400–499 Language
500–599 Pure sciences
600–699 Technology (Applied science)
700–799 The arts
800–899 Literature and rhetoric
900–999 General geography and history

Each of these divisions is subdivided into groups of ten numbers according to the elements within a subject area (see Figure 6). Each group of

# H

## SOCIOLOGY

**HM**    Sociology (General and theoretical)

        101–121    Civilization.  Culture.  Progress
                Cf. CB

        201–219    Social elements, forces, laws

        251–299    Social psychology

**HN**    Social history.  Social reform

        30–39    The church and social problems
              Cf. BR 115.S6

    Social groups

**HQ**    Family.  Marriage.  Home

        16– 471    Sex relations

        750– 799    Eugenics.  Child culture, study, etc.

        1101–1870    Woman.  Feminism

        1871–2030    Women's clubs

**HS**    Associations: Secret societies, clubs, etc.

**HT**    Communities.  Classes.  Races

        101– 381    Urban groups: The city

        401– 485    Rural groups: The country

        851–1445    Slavery
              Works on slavery in the United States of America are
              classified in E441–453.

**HV**    Social pathology.  Philanthropy.  Charities and corrections

        530– 696    Social welfare

        697–4630    Protection, assistance and relief of special classes
              according to age, defects, race, occupation, etc.

        4701–4959    Protection of animals

        4961–4998    Degeneration

        5001–5720    Alcoholism.  Intemperance.  Temperance reform

        5725–5840    Tobacco and drug habits

        6001–6249    Criminology (General)

        6251–7220    Crimes and offenses

        7231–9920    Penology

        7551–8280      Police.  Detectives.  Constabulary

        8301–9920      Prisons.  Penitentiaries.  Punishment and reform

**HX**    Socialism.  Communism.  Anarchism.  Bolshevism

        806–811    Utopias

[8]

Fig. 5    Page 8 from the *Outline of the Library of Congress Classification*, showing letter combinations with numbers for further subdivisions. (Washington, D.C., 1942; reprinted 1962. Reproduced with permission of the Library of Congress.)

## Second Summary
## The 100 Divisions

| 000 | Generalities | 500 | Pure sciences |
|-----|--------------|-----|---------------|
| 010 | Bibliographies & catalogs | 510 | Mathematics |
| 020 | Library science | 520 | Astronomy & allied sciences |
| 030 | General encyclopedic works | 530 | Physics |
| 040 | | 540 | Chemistry & allied sciences |
| 050 | General periodicals | 550 | Earth sciences |
| 060 | General organizations | 560 | Paleontology |
| 070 | Newspapers & journalism | 570 | Anthropolog. & biol. sciences |
| 080 | General collections | 580 | Botanical sciences |
| 090 | Manuscripts & book rarities | 590 | Zoological sciences |
| 100 | Philosophy & related | 600 | Technology (Applied sci.) |
| 110 | Ontology & methodology | 610 | Medical sciences |
| 120 | Knowledge, cause, purpose, man | 620 | Engineering & allied operations |
| 130 | Pseudo- & parapsychology | 630 | Agriculture & agric. industries |
| 140 | Specific philosophic viewpoints | 640 | Domestic arts & sciences |
| 150 | Psychology | 650 | Business & related enterprises |
| 160 | Logic | 660 | Chemical technology etc. |
| 170 | Ethics (Moral philosophy) | 670 | Manufactures processible |
| 180 | Ancient, med., Oriental philos. | 680 | Assembled & final products |
| 190 | Modern Western philosophy | 690 | Buildings |
| 200 | Religion | 700 | The arts |
| 210 | Natural religion | 710 | Civic & landscape art |
| 220 | Bible | 720 | Architecture |
| 230 | Christian doctrinal theology | 730 | Sculpture & the plastic arts |
| 240 | Christ. moral & devotional theol. | 740 | Drawing & decorative arts |
| 250 | Christ. pastoral, parochial, etc. | 750 | Painting & paintings |
| 260 | Christ. social & eccles. theol. | 760 | Graphic arts |
| 270 | Hist. & geog. of Chr. church | 770 | Photography & photographs |
| 280 | Christ. denominations & sects | 780 | Music |
| 290 | Other religions & compar. rel. | 790 | Recreation (Recreational arts) |
| 300 | The social sciences | 800 | Literature & rhetoric |
| 310 | Statistical method & statistics | 810 | American literature in English |
| 320 | Political science | 820 | Engl. & Anglo-Saxon literature |
| 330 | Economics | 830 | Germanic languages literature |
| 340 | Law | 840 | French, Provençal, Catalan lit. |
| 350 | Public administration | 850 | Italian, Romanian etc. literature |
| 360 | Welfare & association | 860 | Spanish & Portuguese literature |
| 370 | Education | 870 | Italic languages literature |
| 380 | Commerce | 880 | Classical & Greek literature |
| 390 | Customs & folklore | 890 | Lits. of other languages |
| 400 | Language | 900 | General geog. & history etc. |
| 410 | Linguistics & nonverbal lang. | 910 | General geography |
| 420 | English & Anglo-Saxon | 920 | General biog., geneal., etc. |
| 430 | Germanic languages | 930 | Gen. hist. of ancient world |
| 440 | French, Provençal, Catalan | 940 | Gen. hist. of modern Europe |
| 450 | Italian, Romanian, etc. | 950 | Gen. hist. of modern Asia |
| 460 | Spanish & Portuguese | 960 | Gen. hist. of modern Africa |
| 470 | Italic languages | 970 | Gen. hist. of North America |
| 480 | Classical & Greek | 980 | Gen. hist. of South America |
| 490 | Other languages | 990 | Gen. hist. of rest of world |

*110*

Fig. 6   Page 110 from the *Dewey Decimal Classification and Relative Index.* (Edition 17, 1965, Vol. 1. Reproduced by permission of Forest Press, Inc., owners of the Copyright.)

ten is further divided in order to accommodate books of greater speciali-zation (see Figure 7). From among all these divisions and subdivisions you should be able to choose a topic or general area. But obviously a selection made on the basis of the secondary or even the tertiary Dewey Decimal Classification division is unworkable. You would certainly not presume to write of "South American History" or "Reptiles and Birds"; these are topics for books, not for student papers. The next chapter explains how you can narrow such a broad topic to a single subject you can handle successfully.

## Topics to Avoid

In order to avoid wasting time and effort, you ought to know that certain kinds of topics are unsuitable for research papers and should not be used.

(1)  *Do not reuse a paper you have written for another instructor.* Repetition does not produce new learning. Besides, to pretend you have done new work when, in fact, you have not done any is dishonest.

Some instructors are willing to let you continue studying something you have already begun investigating provided the topic warrants further research. Or they are willing to let you examine another aspect of a topic about which you have already written a paper. Neither of these situations is the same as handing in to one instructor a paper you have already written and turned in to someone else. However, if you do want to use a previously submitted research paper as the *basis* for a new one, it is safest to discuss the matter frankly with your present instructor.

(2)  *Any topic on which someone else has done your work for you— either the research or the writing—is unacceptable.* Using material in this form without proper acknowledgment is plagiarism.

(3)  *Do not choose a topic if a single source provides all the infor-mation you will need.* You can develop an individual viewpoint, use investigative resources, evaluate materials, and organize your findings in an original way *only* when you consult several sources for information. In short, you can follow the procedures for scholarly research only if you read and study widely.

Remember, too, that the research paper has been partially defined as "a synthesis of your discoveries about a topic" and using a single source does not allow for synthesis. (Only a report can result from using one source.)

(4)  *Avoid choosing a topic about which your conclusions will be*

# Pure sciences

| | | | | |
|---|---|---|---|---|
| **500** | **Pure sciences** | | **550** | **Earth sciences** |
| 501 | Philosophy & theory | | 551 | Physical & dynamic geology |
| 502 | Miscellany | | 552 | Petrology |
| 503 | Dictionaries, encyclopedias, etc. | | 553 | Economic geology |
| 504 | | | 554 | Geology of Europe |
| 505 | Serial publications | | 555 | Geology of Asia |
| 506 | Organizations | | 556 | Geology of Africa |
| 507 | Study & teaching | | 557 | Geology of North America |
| 508 | Collections, travels, surveys | | 558 | Geology of South America |
| 509 | Hist. & geographical treatment | | 559 | Geology of other parts of world |
| **510** | **Mathematics** | | **560** | **Paleontology** |
| 511 | Arithmetic | | 561 | Paleobotany |
| 512 | Algebra | | 562 | Invertebrate paleozoology |
| 513 | Synthetic geometry | | 563 | Protozoa, Parazoa, Metazoa |
| 514 | Trigonometry | | 564 | Mollusca & molluscoidea |
| 515 | Descriptive geometry | | 565 | Other invertebrates |
| 516 | Analytic (Coordinate) geometry | | 566 | Vertebrate paleozoology |
| 517 | Calculus | | 567 | Anamnia (Fishes etc.) |
| 518 | | | 568 | Sauropsida (Reptiles & birds) |
| 519 | Probabilities & statistical math. | | 569 | Mammalia (Mammals) |
| **520** | **Astronomy & allied sci.** | | **570** | **Anthropol. & biological sci.** |
| 521 | Theoretical astronomy | | 571 | |
| 522 | Practical & spherical astronomy | | 572 | Human races (Ethnology) |
| 523 | Descriptive astronomy | | 573 | Somatology (Phys. anthropol.) |
| 524 | | | 574 | Biology |
| 525 | Earth (Astronomical geography) | | 575 | Organic evolution |
| 526 | Mathematical geography | | 576 | Microbiology |
| 527 | Celestial navigation | | 577 | Gen. properties of living matter |
| 528 | Ephemerides (Naut. almanacs) | | 578 | Microscopes & microscopy |
| 529 | Chronology | | 579 | Coll. & preservation of specimens |
| **530** | **Physics** | | **580** | **Botanical sciences** |
| 531 | Mechanics | | 581 | Botany |
| 532 | Mechanics of fluids | | 582 | Spermatophyta |
| 533 | Mechanics of gases | | 583 | Dicotyledones |
| 534 | Sound & related vibrations | | 584 | Monocotyledones |
| 535 | Visible light etc. | | 585 | Gymnospermae |
| 536 | Heat | | 586 | Cryptogamia |
| 537 | Electricity & electronics | | 587 | Pteridophyta |
| 538 | Magnetism | | 588 | Bryophyta |
| 539 | Modern physics | | 589 | Thallophyta |
| **540** | **Chemistry & allied sciences** | | **590** | **Zoological sciences** |
| 541 | Physical & theoret. chemistry | | 591 | Zoology |
| 542 | Laboratories & equipment | | 592 | Invertebrates |
| 543 | General analytical chemistry | | 593 | Protozoa, Parazoa, Metazoa |
| 544 | Qualitative analytical chemistry | | 594 | Mollusca & molluscoidea |
| 545 | Quantitative analytical chemistry | | 595 | Other invertebrates |
| 546 | Inorganic chemistry | | 596 | Chordata (Vertebrates) |
| 547 | Organic chemistry | | 597 | Anamnia (Fishes etc.) |
| 548 | Crystallography | | 598 | Reptiles & birds |
| 549 | Mineralogy | | 599 | Mammalia (Mammals) |

*116*

Fig. 7 Page 116 of the *Dewey Decimal Classification and Relative Index.* (Edition 17, 1965, Vol. 1. Reproduced by permission of Forest Press, Inc., owners of the Copyright.)

*irrelevant.* It would not be particularly fruitful to undertake a paper titled "How Ford Should Have Designed the Edsel [Automobile]" because it does not particularly matter now. (Another sort of investigation about the Edsel might, however, have some value.)

(5)    *Do not start work on any topic unless you think it will hold your interest long enough to complete the paper.* Research is a difficult assignment in itself; if you have to fight boredom with your own topic along the way, it becomes impossible.

(6)    *Be wary of choosing a topic so "neutral" that you cannot express an attitude toward it.* Unless you plan no more than a simple factual report—and not a research paper—you will need to express some opinions about your material. "Commercial By-Products of the Fishing Industry," for instance, hardly suggests any particular viewpoint you could take. Straight biography is also reportorial, for there is little you can add to the facts of someone's life.

(7)    *Some highly controversial topics may be unsuitable; undertake research on one only if you are sure your instructor will approve.* Sometimes a topic is unsuited to a certain level of instruction or to a certain course. Some topics may offend the sensibilities of the instructor or other readers. Or you may find that time or length limitations on the paper will not allow you to present sufficient material to cover a controversial topic adequately. If you have any doubts about the advisability of working on a topic, discuss the matter with your instructor.

(8)    *Consider avoiding topics that have been so popular among students that your instructor may be tired of reading papers about them* —unless they reflect a special interest you have or you can give a special slant to the study. Abortion, marijuana, drugs, and pollution have been popular on many campuses in recent years. Check with your instructor if in doubt about the advisability of researching a particular topic.

(9)    *Do not pursue a topic that seems to "go nowhere" for you.* If you have great trouble narrowing a topic to a manageable subject or finding an approach to a subject (see Chapter 3) , perhaps that topic will prove unproductive for you. Drop it and go on to something you can work with.

# 3
## Narrowing the Topic

Once you have decided on a topic for study, you need to narrow it to a *specific subject* before starting to gather information. It would be foolish to start searching for material on the CIA, for example, before deciding what aspect of that governmental agency you want to investigate; too much time would be wasted unless you knew in advance—or decided very quickly after some preliminary reading—that you were interested in "The CIA and the U-2 Plane," or "The CIA's Role in the Bay of Pigs Invasion," or "Congressional Charges of CIA Intervention in the Politics of [name a country]."

Keep two things in mind as you narrow your topic down to a single subject you can deal with: (1) the required length of the paper you will write, and (2) the source materials available.

(1) You can choose a broader topic for a 2,500-word paper than you can for one of 1,000 words. Since you will want to deal *adequately* with whatever subject you choose, you will need to be guided by the length you plan to write. If your assignment for the research paper does not include a statement of expected length, you will have to use your own judgment about the sort of work you expect of yourself, the time available to fulfill the assignment, and the importance you and your instructor put on the individual research paper. (As noted on p. 4, this book assumes that you are preparing a research paper of from 1,500 to 3,000 words or about six to twelve typewritten pages. Use your judgment, based on time and expectations, for papers of other length.)

The subject you arrive at, after narrowing down a topic, should be neither too broad nor too narrow, and should have both sufficient range and sufficient depth to show that your work is that of a serious student. Do not choose a subject so broad that you must be superficial in order to fit it into the required length. (The topic "Modern American Writers" may be narrowed down to "Arthur Miller," but even that is suited only to a book-length study. Even "Arthur Miller as a Playwright" is too broad a subject for an adequate treatment in 3,000 words.) Nor should you choose a subject so specialized or esoteric that you need to present a great deal of background information before you begin to write about the topic itself. ("How Rhodopsin is Related to the Breakdown of the Visual Purple of the Eye" is a good subject choice for only the most specialized science course.)

(2)    Libraries try to supply the particular needs of their users, so they all have certain limitations. A library in a residential community would probably have more fiction books than research materials; one in a school devoted primarily to science or engineering courses may not have enough materials on art or music to make research on those subjects convenient. Using highly specialized libraries, relatively new ones, or those not able to make adequate new purchases may hamper your research work. If you want to make a study of flood control in Ohio and the latest information available in the library is dated 1960, or if you want to find criticism on *Lazarillo de Tormes* and discover that it is available only in Spanish—which you do not read—you ought to choose another topic for investigation. In other words, you must have sufficient research sources readily available for your study, and not all libraries are adequate for all projects. (School libraries, though, usually try to have sufficient materials for the work of most students, and there may be other or specialized libraries in the community or nearby that can augment what you have most readily available.)

If you choose too narrow a topic, you may find that your library lacks the information you need for a paper of the length demanded. "Abalone Harvesting off Carmel" would probably be too narrow even for most California libraries, but "Abalone in the Ecology and Economy of California" might yield sufficient information for study, even outside California.

Before you decide definitely on a subject for your research, know what is available in the library or libraries you plan to use and, if necessary, adjust the scope of the subject to fit the resources you will have to work from.

Not all research materials need to come from libraries (as will be explained in Chapter 4). But if you plan to use other sources, such as letters of inquiry or interviews, be sure there is sufficient time to receive responses or hold the interviews before deciding on the specific subject so that you will have the materials needed to work from.

## Focusing on a Subject for Research

After you have selected a suitable topic for your research paper, you next need to narrow it down to a specific subject to investigate. Occasionally the choice of topic immediately brings to mind a specific subject and thus there is no problem. But if you are one of the many students who has trouble narrowing a topic down to a workable subject, you may find useful three methods that have already proved helpful to students: **subdividing, free association,** and the **five Ws.**

### Subdividing

One way to narrow a topic is to write down the general area you have selected and then divide it into progressively smaller units, dividing and subdividing until you reach a subject you are interested in researching.

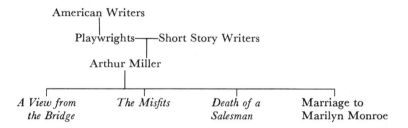

Or, consider this example of subdividing:

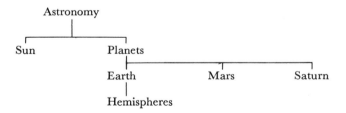

From this point you could proceed in several ways. You might choose to research information sent back about Mars from the Viking landers. Or you might deal with Mars as viewed by one or more science fiction writers. Perhaps you will deal with the scientific accuracy of a fiction writer's information about Mars. Pursuing another line of study, you might divide "Hemispheres" into progressively smaller units: Southern Hemisphere, South America, Peru, and so on.

You can easily use this method of subdividing to choose a Field-of-Study subject for research. Suppose your paper had to be related to geology; you could subdivide "Hemispheres" into "Continents" and you might investigate a specific geological formation on the North American continent, the San Andreas Fault.

## Free Association

Another way of narrowing your research topic is to write down the general area you have decided to study and then practice a kind of brainstorming called "free association," writing down everything about the subject that comes to mind. For instance:

**Ships**

    transportation
    racing craft
    Operation Sail, July 4, 1976
    private craft
    personal pleasures
    different sizes
    motorboats
    sailboats
    lure of—Joseph Conrad
    whaling

From this list you can choose a specific subject. Suppose it is "racing craft."

Your next step is to search out information from the library on racing ships. If you didn't already know it before going to the library, you would then discover that the subject is still too large to be dealt with adequately in the assigned number of words (books are written about racing ships—a sure sign it is too broad a subject for a school research paper). Further narrowing is in order, and you may do that either by association or by subdividing. Suppose you decided to limit the study to sailboat racing. You might have to focus even more narrowly and research racing sailboats, but neither of the two methods so far explained seems to be helpful for further narrowing. For further narrowing, another method (illustrated in the next section) can be used.

## The Five Ws

A third way of narrowing and focusing a topic adapts the journalistic idea that good reporting means covering the five Ws of a story: who, what, where, when, and why. These key words guide the complete coverage of a subject being reported, so by using them as guides to a given topic, they can help you find a useful research subject.

Who—people
What—problems, things, ideas
Where—places
When—past, present, future
Why—causes, reasons, results, conditions

To use these five Ws as a help in finding a research subject, write the name of your topic at the top of a page and under it write each of the Ws as headings across the page. Then, use free association with the key word that heads each column to find ideas for research. "Crime" is certainly a very general topic, but specific research subjects can be arrived at in this way:

### Example 1  (from General Topic to Research Subject)

**Crime**

| *Who* | *What* | *Where* | *When* | *Why* |
|---|---|---|---|---|
| victims | locking up houses | in specific city | at present time | contributing conditions |
| famous criminals | effect of publicity | national | in the 1890s | changes made in population distribution |
| first offenders | prevention | international | after dark | |
| professionals | role of police | in England | daylight | overcrowded jails |
| informers | rehabilitation | in South Seas | | legal problems |
| | bail system | | | |

Some topics arrived at in this fashion are still too broad to be suitable for research. "Crime in England," for instance, encompasses many people over a long period and therefore will not do for a research paper. But it can be narrowed further by the same five-Ws method.

### Crime in England

| Who | What | Where | When | Why |
|---|---|---|---|---|
| Jack the Ripper | famous murders | London | 18th century | relation to police not carrying guns |
| Bluebeard | bank robberies | outlying towns | 19th century | "profile" of criminals |
| Sherlock Holmes | Scotland Yard involvement | | 20th century | |
| prototypical criminal | | | postwar resurgence of Irish nationalism in the 1950s | |

By this further use of the five Ws, you might find a subject of interest such as "The Relationship between British Police Arming and Crime" (a longer paper might give you a chance to compare this relationship in England to the same relationship in the United States) or "Irish Nationalist Retaliatory Bombing in England Since 1960" or "Sherlock Holmes as the Ideal 'Gentleman Detective.'"

As already indicated, it is possible to combine methods of focusing on a subject for research. Since "Racing Sailboats" is too broad to write about, and if neither subdividing nor free association helps narrow the subject, you could try the five-Ws method.

### Example 2 (from Partially Narrowed Topic)

### Racing Sailboats

| Who | What | Where | When | Why |
|---|---|---|---|---|
| designers | kinds | famous races | origin of America's Cup | crew as factor in winning races |
| famous skippers | sail-making | racing areas in U.S. or Europe | current innovative designs | |

If enough source material were available, any one of these items could serve as your research subject. Should your choice prove difficult to work from, try combining two or more related ideas, such as "designers" and "current innovative designs" or "famous races" and "racing areas."

# Finding an Approach

Once you decide on a subject that you can treat adequately in the assigned length and about which you can find sufficient material, you must decide on only one more aspect before you are ready to begin collecting information: the approach you will take towards your subject. Some preliminary reading may help and for that you might look at an encyclopedia, some books found through the card catalog (see Chapter 4), or a few periodical articles located through an appropriate index. But you should not do a great deal of reading or notetaking until you do decide on an approach to your subject because you will want to make the best use of your time.

Finding an approach does *not* mean that you decide in advance what your paper will contain or what you expect to learn from a study. Rather, it means that you determine in advance of collecting information the *method* you will use to deal with the material—and you will then know what to look for. (The approach you use will also help with the organization of your paper when it is time to write it.) For example, for the sample research paper in Appendix C, a paper relating Arthur Miller's versions of "The Misfits" (which was subsequently written as a movie script for his wife, Marilyn Monroe, and Clark Gable), the approach decided on was to *relate* versions of the story. The student, therefore, did not waste time in researching Miller's plays, or his other short stories, or his personal life.

As you read about the kinds of approaches you might take toward your subject, note that many of the sample titles in this book have two parts—the subject and the approach. Thus, *The Misfits* is the subject of the sample paper, but the approach is to examine versions of the story. "Obesity" is a subject one can research, but the approach is reflected in the rest of the title of a possible research paper on the subject: "Some Ways to Overcome Obesity." *"Peter Rabbit* in Story and Film" and "Mica Mining Techniques to Meet Commercial Demands" also show that the subject, italicized in each illustration, needs to have an approach.

Also, note that none of these sample subjects or the approaches illustrated is in the form of a question. To phrase the subject in that fashion only serves to confuse you when you begin collecting information. Thus "How Has Richard III Been Depicted?" should be rephrased in a two-part statement that gives both subject and approach: "Richard III as Depicted by Shakespeare and by Twentieth-Century Historians." Should you have a question in mind as you think about the approach, simply turn it into a phrase that states the approach you can take toward a subject.

There are four general approaches you might take toward your subject:

1. You can **examine** it, looking at various aspects of the subject and viewing it from more than one perspective.

2. You can **compare and/or contrast** things or ideas, showing how both similarities and dissimilarities exist or are evident to one looking closely at the subject.

3. You can **establish relationships** among ideas, showing how they may have drawn from each other or otherwise evidenced similarity.

4. You can **argue for or against something** and try to persuade readers to agree with you.

As you will note in the following explanations and examples, it is not always possible to make clear-cut distinctions among the four ways of approaching a topic. A paper that is concerned essentially with *examining* a subject may also involve some *comparison. Comparison and contrast* are both types of *relationships.* However, if you decide upon an essential approach to your subject at the outset, you will find it easy to work purposefully and gather only related material.

### Examining

Examining a subject is like putting it under a microscope to see the details that comprise it. You can examine anything from a single event to an entire political or scientific theory, looking at it closely enough to see how it is put together or what constitute its parts. You might examine the stylistic devices in a work of literature (*"Tom Jones* as a Picaresque Novel," "Mythological Allusion in the *Inferno"*) ; the intellectual, scientific, or sociological background of a person or time ("The Labor Union Movement in Golda Meir's Youth," "Wartime Needs for Underwater Exploration") ; the variations or revisions of a work of art ("Development of *Guernica* Based on Picasso's Sketches," "Versions of 'Sailing to Byzantium' ") ; the evolution of a business practice ("Selling Door-to-Door Magazine Subscriptions," "Growth of the Credit Card Industry") ; and other subjects. To research "Graham Greene as a Movie Critic," "British Child-Labor Laws during the Industrial Revolution," "Lumalox as a New Lighting Technique," "Political Influences on Participation of Countries in the Modern Olympic Games," "Nursing Care for Terminal Patients," "Cost Factors in Industrial Solar Heating," or "The Influence of Numerology on Medieval Church Architecture" is, in each case, to choose an approach that examines the subject.

Evaluation or criticism is another aspect of examining a subject since you cannot judge anything until you have looked at it carefully. Literature is often the subject of critical analysis in research papers ("The Role of the Brother in *The Glass Menagerie*," "Dorothy Parker as Spokesperson for Women"). Many research papers are evaluations of individuals, works, or ideas ("The Effectiveness of the NRA," "Rachel Carson's Writings and Ecological Awareness").

### Comparing and Contrasting

Although the two words define different approaches—to compare is to find similarities, to contrast is to find differences—they are often used together in order to give a fuller view of the subject than one alone might provide. If you use either or both of these methods, however, you must be sure there is some basis for the comparison or the contrast of ideas, people, works, or materials; things compared or contrasted usually have qualities or characteristics in common. For instance, Republican and Democratic platforms during national election years differ, but they can be compared and contrasted because each puts forth the bases upon which members of the party seek election.

You might compare criticisms of a work ("How *QB VII* Was Received by the Critics"), or of individuals ("Views of Harry Truman as a President") or of ideas ("The Taft-Hartley Act as Seen by Contemporary Critics"). You can compare or contrast events as viewed by different countries ("Israeli and Arab Views of the Six-Day War") or as viewed by people in different situations ("The Revolutionary War as Seen by Loyalists Who Stayed in the Colonies and Those Who Didn't"). Describing changing views or similar views toward a person, idea, or event are other comparison and contrast approaches to a research subject.

Some examples of the sorts of subjects you might choose to approach by comparison and contrast are "Unappreciative Daughters in Shakespeare and Balzac," "Economy Facts in Gas Turbine and Piston Auto Engines," "Educational Ideas of Montaigne and Dewey," "*High Noon* and *Shane* as Archetypal Western Films," "Translations of *Faust* by Kaufmann, Raphael, and Wayne," "Don Quixote and Batman," "Nutritional Values of Three Popular Diets."

### Relating

Establishing relationships among ideas is primary to comprehension and, therefore, an essential part of education. A research work that establishes or explores relationships requires you to exercise much perception and is, therefore, very challenging, but this kind of study is one of the most rewarding you can undertake.

As you think back over what has already been stated about comparison and contrast (and, to a lesser extent, about examining as an approach), you will see that both approaches are kinds of relationships. But, in determining an approach for research, it is also helpful to consider the relating of ideas as a distinctive kind of approach.

You might show the relationship between a theory and its practical application ("The Psychology of the Underdog in 'Peanuts'") or the relationship between a person's work or thought and life ("Martin Luther King, Jr., as an Effective Leader of Civil Rights Activists"). Or, you could relate an individual to a specific event or attitude ("John Steinbeck and Social Consciousness").

Other research subjects that use the approach of establishing relationships are: "The Morality of Listening Devices," "Mendelian Theory in the Selective Breeding of Cattle," "The Search for Adequate Written Characters for Spoken Eskimo Languages," "Productive Working Environments," "*La Raza* as Social, Political, and Economic Rallying Point."

## Arguing

When you try to persuade someone to believe or act in a particular way, you are arguing for belief or action. At the heart of persuasive writing is the orderly presentation of the factual materials and information that make your case believable; so argumentation is often an approach used for research papers. You might want to write a research paper that defends a position ("The U.S. Had to Become Involved in Vietnam," "Nobel Literature Prizes Are Often Conferred for Political Rather Than Literary Reasons"); one that justifies an action ("Frequent Auto Design Changes *Are* Necessary"); or one that seeks to prove a belief ("*Candide* Is as Current Today as It Was When Voltaire Wrote It," "Common Stocks of Companies X and Y as Good Investments"). The thesis of each might be worded differently from these titles, but the approach would be to argue a point of view.

Once a subject and an approach to it have been decided upon, you will find it easy to collect information for your research paper because you will know exactly what you need to look for. And should you find that you misjudged in the approach, that it is proving infeasible, you can quickly find another based on your early information-gathering.

# 4

## Collecting Information

### Primary and Secondary Sources

A good research paper relies on primary source material when it is available, and on both primary and secondary sources when possible. A paper is likely to lose credibility if only secondary sources are used for information.

**Primary sources** are the most direct kind of information. If you are writing about literature or the arts, the works of art are your primary sources: novels, short stories, poems, plays, films, paintings, sculpture, and so on. Diaries, notes, letters, and autobiographies are other kinds of primary materials. Interviews made by a market researcher, observations of an astronomer, a music historian relating the circumstances of the discovery of a newfound Mozart manuscript—all these are primary sources. If you want to know what the president of the United States believes about foreign policy, go directly to his speeches and writings. Neil Armstrong's report of his moon walk is a primary source—and is more reliable than someone else's report of the event. Do not overlook public documents as primary sources: *The Congressional Record,* the *U.S. Census Reports,* and so on are helpful.

Primary sources are not always easy to find, particularly in the limited time you have for most research assignments. Sometimes they are impossible to locate, and you may be forced to depend entirely on secondary sources. But you can always use your ingenuity. For instance, as a primary source for research on "The Effectiveness of the City of X's Water Supply System for Fire Fighting," you might interview or correspond with some of the people responsible for drawing up the master plan for the water supply and with some of the fire fighters who have had to rely on that water supply. Or you might correspond with the manufacturer of a pollution control device newly installed by a company in your city to obtain information about its development and to get leads to other companies that have used it and can tell you about its effectiveness and costs.

**Secondary sources** are one step removed from the original and are often an evaluation, commentary, or summary of primary materials. Helpful as they are, they need to be considered for what they are: the writings of another person on a subject. Therefore, they will probably show the biases of the author, just as your own research paper will probably reflect your own bias.

The short story, "The Misfits," and the book-length version of the story, which is a novelization of the film script *The Misfits,* are primary sources for the research paper in Appendix C. Some of the secondary sources used are Shiela Huftel's book, *Arthur Miller: The Burning Glass* and Henry Popkin's article in *Commentary,* "Arthur Miller Out West." (See the sample research paper for the correct acknowledgment form of these sources.)

Other examples of secondary source material are Carl Sandburg's books about Abraham Lincoln (Lincoln's own letters and speeches as well as documents of the period are the primary sources upon which they were based), a newspaper reporter's account of misuse of government funds (reports and other records of disbursements together with statements from the people involved are the primary sources), and a summary of investigations of extraterrestrial soil samples (actual reports of the tests are the primary sources).

Although secondary sources are useful, there is danger in relying too heavily on them, especially if you ignore the materials on which they are based. You should, therefore, check on them carefully by going back to the original (primary) source when possible, by viewing the materials skeptically and critically, and by learning something about the authors as a way of judging veracity, reliability, or bias. Then you will have a clearer picture of the usefulness of the secondary sources to your own gathering of research information.

## Where to Find Information

The reference room of your library is the starting place to collect information for your research paper. If you have not already looked in indexes and encyclopedias when looking for a topic to study, you will have a chance to look at them now in specific ways. You are probably already familiar with the card catalog and with one of the more popular periodical indexes, the *Readers' Guide to Periodical Literature.* But there are many more sources than these to consult—and the more sources you use, the easier it is to find materials that will make your research paper a good one. For instance, since the *Readers' Guide* lists only articles in popular, mass-audience magazines, it may not prove very helpful for a paper on student ratings of teachers; the *Education Index* would probably have more relevant entries.

Begin searching for information by locating useful books through the card catalog, because books usually provide a broad view of your chosen subject and thus will give you a general look at the subject you are researching. Look through encyclopedia entries if any are relevant to your subject. Next, look at appropriate periodical indexes to find articles you can read for details on your chosen subject. Then go on to the additional sources such as audiovisual materials, interviews, the vertical file index, and others you will find noted later in this chapter.

As you look for information on your subject, make a preliminary bibliography card for each likely looking source. You can quickly discover if a book has any content on your subject by skimming the table of contents and the index, by glancing at articles located through periodical and other indexes, or by judging from the titles of works. If you were looking for material on "The Misfits," for instance, you would not spend time noting bibliography cards or seeking books or articles on Arthur Miller's plays (because "The Misfits" was a story, novel, and motion picture).

### The Card Catalog

Every book in a library's collection is listed in its card catalog. Non-fiction books are entered on three separate cards: one headed by the author's name, one by the book title, and one by the subject. There may also be additional cards headed by an alternate subject, by a story title within a book of collected stories, by a translator, by a writer's pseudonym, and so on. Since catalog cards are made to help locate information, they are headed in as many ways as possible to aid you.

Fiction books are listed on separate cards by title and by author's name.

Each of these 3 x 5-inch cards is then filed, according to the heading, in card catalog drawers with an alphabetical notation on the outside of each one to show its contents.

Some libraries have a **dictionary catalog.** In this type of catalog all holdings are listed in alphabetical order according to card headings. Thus, you would be able to find "Miller, Arthur" very near *"Misfits, The."*

Other libraries have a **divided catalog.** This card catalog is divided into separate sections, one each for author, title, and subject cards. (Obviously fiction books appear only in the author and title sections.) Nonfiction books may appear in more than one place in the subject section; for instance, a book about trees might also be listed under "forestry" and "ecology."

Some libraries now have printed catalogs instead of the more familiar card files. The printed catalog is a bound volume that looks like a large book. Inside are reproduced the same Library of Congress cards that would otherwise be found in the traditional drawers of cards.

**Author Card**    The "author card" is basic to the catalog and is the prime entry card for each book in a library (see Figure 8). When a book

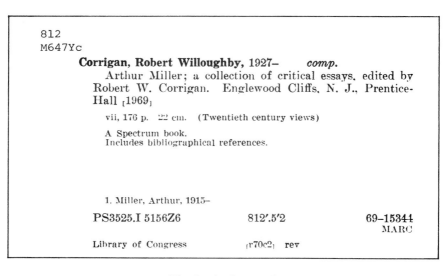

Fig. 8   Author card.

is published, copies of it are sent to the Library of Congress in Washington and the author card is printed. Libraries make their own title, subject, and other heading cards by typing the appropriate information above the author's name. Each also adds its own designations—the numbers of the Dewey Decimal Classification system or the letters of the Library of Congress cataloging system—on the top left corner of the card to show the location of the book in the library.

**Title Card**    The "title card" for both fiction and nonfiction is the basic author card but with the book title typed in black ink at the top of the card, above the author's name. (see Figure 9). It is filed in alphabetical order in dictionary catalogs and alphabetically with other title cards in divided catalogs. Titles that begin with "a," "an" or "the" are alpha-

```
812
M647Yc     Arthur Miller
```
**Corrigan, Robert Willoughby,** 1927–    *comp.*
> Arthur Miller; a collection of critical essays, edited by
> Robert W. Corrigan.  Englewood Cliffs, N. J., Prentice-
> Hall ₁1969₎
>
> vii, 176 p.  22 cm.  (Twentieth century views)
>
> A Spectrum book.
> Includes bibliographical references.
>
>
> 1. Miller, Arthur, 1915–

```
PS3525.I 5156Z6          812'.5'2                69–15344
                                                   MARC
```
```
Library of Congress        ₁r70c2₎  rev
```

Fig. 9   Title card.

betized by the second word, and the article is shown following a comma
at the end of the title. As with the author card, the library call number
or letter appears on the top left corner of the title card.

**Subject Card**   Nonfiction books are listed in one or more subject
locations in the card catalog. The subject under which the card is filed

```
812
M647Yc     Miller, Arthur, 1915–
```
**Corrigan, Robert Willoughby,** 1927–    *comp.*
> Arthur Miller; a collection of critical essays, edited by
> Robert W. Corrigan.  Englewood Cliffs, N. J., Prentice-
> Hall ₁1969₎
>
> vii, 176 p.  22 cm.  (Twentieth century views)
>
> A Spectrum book.
> Includes bibliographical references.
>
>
> 1. Miller, Arthur, 1915–

```
PS3525.I 5156Z6          812'.5'2                69–15344
                                                   MARC
```
```
Library of Congress        ₁r70c2₎  rev
```

Fig. 10   Subject card.

is typed, usually in red ink, above the author's name on an "author card" (see Figure 10). A book will have as many subject cards as it has subjects under which it is listed. The call number or letter is also typed on each subject card.

**"See also" Cards**    The helpful "See also" reference cards (see Figure 3, pp. 18–19) are in the card catalog at the end of a subject section. Sometimes they lead to important information, so it is wise not to overlook them.

**Catalog Customs**    Here are some uniform practices of library cataloging that will help you find materials easily:

(1)    Abbreviations such as *St., Dr., U.S.,* and *19th cent.* are filed as if they were spelled out: "Saint," "Doctor," "United States," and "Nineteenth century." If you were looking for the book *St. Thomas and the Future of Metaphysics* by Joseph Owens, you would turn to "Saint Thomas . . ." in the card catalog.

(2)    Filing is alphabetical word by word and letter by letter *to the end of each word.* It is not simply a letter-by-letter listing. For example, the proper catalog order is:

| | |
|---|---|
| North Carolina | *Not:*    North Carolina |
| North Dakota | Northcote |
| Northcote | North Dakota |
| The Northwest Wind | Northwestern |
| Northwestern | The Northwest Wind |

(3)    Names beginning with *Mac, Mc,* or *M'* are all filed as though they began with *Mac.* The cataloging order is:

Mach
McHale
Mac Henry
Machine

(4)    Foreign prefixes such as "de," "van," or "von" are not used when filing; filing is done by last name: Beethoven, Ludwig van. If the "De" or "Van" is part of an English name, however, filing is done by prefix: De Witt, John. Spanish names are filed by patronym (father's family name) rather than by the mother's maiden name or the place name, either of which, according to Spanish custom, is often added to an individual's given name, thus: Cervantes Saavedra, Miguel de.

(5)    Titles are filed according to the first significant word; articles such as "a," "an," "the" (or their foreign equivalents) are written in after the principal words. Thus, *The Misfits,* a book title, is listed under "M" in the card catalog.

(6)    The order of works by and about an individual is this:
a. Books authored.

> Dewey, John. <u>Art</u> <u>as</u> <u>Experience.</u> New York: Minton,
> Balch and Co., 1934.

b. Books co-authored (if the name appears first on the title page).

> Dewey, John, and Arthur F. Bentley. <u>Knowing</u> <u>and</u> <u>the</u>
> <u>Known.</u> Boston: Beacon Press, 1949.

c. Books edited.

> Dewey, John, ed. <u>New</u> <u>York</u> <u>and</u> <u>the</u> <u>Seabury</u> <u>Investi-</u>
> <u>gators.</u> New York: The City Affairs Committee
> of N.Y., 1933.

d. Books about the person.

> Hook, Sidney. <u>John</u> <u>Dewey:</u> <u>An</u> <u>Intellectual</u> <u>Portrait.</u>
> New York: John Day Co., 1939.

e. Books about the person's works.

> Blewett, John. <u>John</u> <u>Dewey:</u> <u>His</u> <u>Thoughts</u> <u>and</u>
> <u>Influence.</u> New York: Fordham University Press,
> 1960.

(7)    Subjects are subdivided in alphabetical order, except for history, which is subdivided in chronological order. For example, catalog cards about "Songs" are divided into these groups, in order: Ballads, Carols, Children's Songs, Drinking Songs, Folk Songs, Madrigals, Popular Songs. Catalog cards about historical eras are divided according to time. Behind a header card on which is printed "Gt. Brit.-History (By Period)" are many eras designated in red type. Among them, in order, are:

Roman Period, 55 BC–449 AD
Anglo-Saxon Period, 449–1066
14th Century
Wars of the Roses—1455–1485

(8)    If the same word is applicable to a person, place, subject, and book title, then, in dictionary catalog filing, the cards follow that same order. (Obviously this practice is not applicable to a divided catalog.) For instance:

Washington, George (the person)
Washington, D.C. (a place)
*Washington Square* (a book title)

## Periodical Indexes

After books, a likely place to seek information is periodicals. By consulting one or more periodical indexes, you will find magazines and newspapers where information about your research subject has been published.

**Magazine Indexes**    Of all the magazine indexes, the *Readers' Guide to Periodical Literature* is probably the best known (see Figure 11). It lists, under author and subject headings, articles appearing in more than one hundred general magazines. Since 1953 it has also listed articles from some scientific magazines although other indexes exist for specialized or technical periodicals. Twenty-two issues of the *Readers' Guide* are published every year. These are put into cumulative index form every three months, and at the end of every odd-numbered year, there is a two-year bound cumulation.

The *Social Sciences Index* and the *Humanities Index* (formerly together and at one time called the *International Index to Periodicals* and later *A Guide to Periodical Literature in the Social Sciences and the Humanities*) are good sources of information about articles in foreign magazines and in magazines more specific or scholarly than those listed in the *Readers' Guide.*

The *Education Index,* the *Art Index,* the *Business Periodicals Index,* the *Applied Science and Technology Index,* and the *Book Review Digest* are among the many specific indexes you can consult, depending on your research subject. (Appendix A contains the titles of many periodical indexes, listed under the subject headings.)

You should also know about the *Cross-Reference Index* because it may help you find information under subject headings you did not think of. It will suggest to you the most appropriate headings from the Library of Congress, *Sears List of Subject Headings, Readers' Guide to Periodical Literature,* the *New York Times Index,* the *Public Affairs Information Service Bulletin,* and *Business Periodical Index.* If you are looking for material on collective bargaining, for example, the *Cross-Reference Index* will refer you to a number of headings in each source (see Figure 12).

SPACE astronomy—*Continued*
Extreme-ultraviolet astronomy from Apollo-Soyuz. B. Margon and S. Bowyer. il Sky & Tel 50:4-9 Jl '75
Skylab and the sun: symposium. il Space World L-10-142:9-33 O '75
*See also*
Rockets—Astronomical use
Space flight—Astronomical use
SPACE biology
Effects of long-term space flight; ASTP medical experiments. Space World L-9-141: 23-4 S '75
Soviet and American scientists meet in Tashkent; joint USSR-US working group on space biology and medicine. E. Khodfa'ev. Space World L-3-135:25 Mr '75
U.S. experiments set for Soviet Vostok. C. Covault. Aviation W 103:20 S 22 '75
SPACE centers
NASA specialists may have been bugged; U.S. personnel at Russia's Kalinin control center. Aviation W 103:17 Ag 11 '75
Two-nation control center plan proved. C. Covault. Aviation W 103:23-4 Jl 28 '75
U.S., Soviet experts support ASTP flight; photographs. Aviation W 103:43-5 Ag 4 '75
*See also*
United States—Lyndon B. Johnson space center
SPACE colonies (proposed)
Cities in the sky. R. Dempewolff. il Pop Mech 143:94-7+ My '75
Colonization of space. G. K. O'Neill; discussion. Phys Today 28:13+ S '75
Colonizing space; theories of G. K. O'Neill. il Time 105:60 My 26 '75
Colonizing the heavens; space cylinders of G. O'Neill. il Sat R 2:12-13+ Je 28 '75
Garden of feasibility. G. Cravens. il Harper 251:66-8+ Ag '75
Humanity unlimited; proposals of G. K. O'Neill. T. Paine. por Newsweek 86:11 Ag 25 '75
Space colonies: home. home on Lagrange. il Sci N 108:149 S 6 '75
Space suburbia; work of Gerard K. O'Neill. il Sci Digest 78:10-11 Ag '75
SPACE committee. See United Nations—Committee on the peaceful uses of outer space
SPACE communication. See Interstellar communication
SPACE cooperation. See Space research—International aspects
SPACE debris. See Space pollution
SPACE exploration. See Space, Outer—Exploration
SPACE flight
Outer planet missions keyed to Centaur. C. Covault. il Aviation W 102:47-9 Je 9 '75
Planners use new shuttle traffic model; plan for shuttle flights from 1980-1991. Aviation W 102:49 My 26 '75
*See also*
Computers—Space flight use
Navigation (space flight)
United States—National aeronautics and space administration

Astronomical use
*See* Space astronomy

International aspects
Crisis in astronautics; address. January 30, 1975. F. E. Moss. Vital Speeches 41:296-8 Mr 1 '75
U.S., USSR differ on future joint flight. il Aviation W 103:20-1 Ag 4 '75
What could Apollo-Soyuz lead to? W. Von Braun. il Pop Sci 206:41 Ja '75
*See also*
Space flight—Manned flights—Apollo-Soyuz flight, 1975
United Nations—Committee on the peaceful uses of outer space

Manned flights
Aleksey Lenov: space walk and space handshake. il pors Space World L-6-138:10-28 Je '75
Cosmonauts: results and plans; interview. V. Shatalov. por Space World L-6-138:34 Je '75
Record of manned space programs; from the first moon landing; chart. U.S. News 79:15 Jl 21 '75
Soviets to solidify manned flight effort. Aviation W 102:71 Mr 17 '75
Valentina Tereshkova—the only woman in space. il pors Space World L-4-136:11-23 Ap '75
*See also*
Astronauts
Orbital rendezvous (space flight)
Space flight to the moon—Manned flights
Space stations—Skylab missions
Space vehicles—Docking systems

*Apollo-Soyuz flight, 1975*
ASTP astronauts avert landing disaster. E. J. Bulban. il Aviation W 103:16-19 Ag 4 '75
ASTP crews begin full-scale practices. Aviation W 102:21 Mr 31 '75
ASTP mission; special report, with editorial comment. il Aviation W 102:11, 36-43+ My 5 '75
ASTP preparations move ahead with major milestones passed; photographs. Aviation W 102:55 F 10 '75
ASTP research spurs medical benefits. C. Covault. Aviation W 103:53 N 17 '75
ASTP's ultraviolet star: new window? Sci N 108:71 Ag 2 '75
All systems go for ASTP. il Sky & Tel 50: 13-14 Jl '75
Apollo and Soyuz crews commended by President Ford before liftoffs; text of message. July 15, 1975. G. R. Ford. Dept State Bull 73:261 Ag 18 '75
Apollo provides mineral detection data. R. G. O'Lone. Aviation W 104:36-7 Ja 5 '76
Apollo-Soyuz. R. Dempewolff. il Pop Mech 143:53-5+ Je '75
Apollo-Soyuz; a dangerous finale. il Time 106: 38 Ag 4 '75
Apollo-Soyuz; appointment in space. il Time 106:53-7 Jl 21 '75
Apollo-Soyuz as news. J. Eberhart. Sci N 108:72 Ag 2 '75
Apollo-Soyuz mission: détente goes orbital. J. N. Wilford. il Sat R 2:14-15 Je 28 '75
Apollo-Soyuz mission successful. Sky & Tel 50:154 S '75
Apollo Soyuz test project: experiments and biographical material. il Space World L-8-140:20-32 Ag '75
Astrodiplomacy in orbit. J. Eberhart. il Sci N 107:10-12 Jl 5 '75
Astronauts' Tyuratam tour restricted; U.S. astronauts first Americans to visit the Soviet Tyuratam launch site. C. Covault. il Aviation W 102:19-21 My 12 '75
Crew cites noise, static in Apollo return. C. Covault. Aviation W 103:16-17 Ag 18 '75
Detente at 140 miles up. J. McWethy. U.S. News 79:34 Jl 14 '75
Effects of long-term space flight; ASTP medical experiments. Space World L-9-141: 23-4 S '75
Extreme-ultraviolet astronomy from Apollo-Soyuz. B. Margon and S. Bowyer. il Sky & Tel 50:4-9 Jl '75
Getting the picture; media coverage. A. R. Martin and others. il Newsweek 86:48 Jl 28 '75
Hands across the heavens. P. Gwynne and others. il Newsweek 86:40-2 Jl 28 '75
Hands all round and four for dinner. il Time 106:34-6 Jl 28 '75
Into space with the Russians. il U.S. News 79:13-14 Jl 21 '75
Language to pose no barrier in Apollo-Soyuz flight. Space World L-9-141:29 S '75
Link-up in space. P. Gwynne and others. il Newsweek 86:46-51 Jl 21 '75
Listen in to Apollo/Soyuz test project. Pop Electr 8:76 Jl '75
Minimal Soyuz 18 impact on ASTP seen. Aviation W 102:14-16 Ap 14 '75
Mission Marooned: effect of novel on Russian participation in Apollo-Soyuz flight. il Time 105:69 Ap 7 '75
More on Apollo-Soyuz. R. N. Watts, Jr. il Sky & Tel 49:91 F '75
Multipurpose furnace to be used for ASTP experiments. Space World L-8-140:33-4 Ag '75
Mystery gas. P. Gwynne and L. Alexander. il Newsweek 86:52 Ag 4 '75
NASA learns Soviet plans in press kit. C. Covault. Aviation W 102:21-2 Je 30 '75
NASA specialists may have been bugged; U.S. personnel at Russia's Kalinin control center. Aviation W 103:17 Ag 11 '75
Next in space: they'll go their separate ways. il U.S. News 79:14-16 Jl 28 '75
No pictures, please; American astronauts training in Russia. Time 105:42 My 12 '75
Picture story of Apollo-Soyuz. J. E. Oberg. il Space World L-7-139:4-15 Jl '75
Second Salyut-4 mission seen no conflict with ASTP flight. Aviation W 102:27-8 Je 2 '75
Soviet-American rendezvous in orbit. G. Reznichenko. Space World L-3-135:24-5 Mr '75
Soviet photos show three views of Apollo. il Aviation W 103:19 O 20 '75
Soviet story of Soyuz-Apollo. il Space World L-11-143:4-28 N '75
Soviets disclose few experimental data. Aviation W 103:38 D 15 '75
Soyuz and Apollo dock on the ground. A. Gorokhov. il Space World L-3-135:24 Mr '75
Soyuz-Apollo; a symbol for history. America 133:45 Ag 2 '75

Fig. 11   Page from the *Readers' Guide to Periodical Literature* showing entries on space subjects. (Copyright © 1975, 1976 by The H. W. Wilson Company. Material reproduced by permission of the publisher.)

**COLLECTIVE BARGAINING**
See also appropriate subd., e.g., Collective bargaining—
      Railroads.

LC      ——; s.a. Arbitration, Industrial; Collective
labor agreements; Labor contract; Labor disputes;
Labor laws and legislation; Management rights;
Mediation and conciliation, Industrial; Negotia-
tion; Trade-unions; Union security; Works
councils

SEARS    ——; s.a. Labor and laboring classes; Labor
contracts; Labor unions; Strikes and lockouts;
Trades and professional associations

RG      ——; s.a. Arbitration, Industrial; Industrial
relations; Trade unions

NYT    ——; s.a. Labor—U.S.—Arbitration, conciliation
and mediation; Labor—U.S.—Strikes; Labor—U.S.
—Unionization

PAIS    ——; s.a. Check-off system; Collective labor
agreements; Employees' representation in
management; Management—Rights and responsi-
bilities; Right to work; subd. *Collective labor
agreements* under subjects

BPI     ——; s.a. Collective labor agreements; Open and
closed shops; Strikes

Fig. 12   Sample of an entry from the *Cross-Reference Index.*

The capital letters in the left column are abbreviations of the various sources cataloged in the *Index.* LC stands for the Library of Congress; in the Library of Congress, subject headings related to collective bargaining may be found under that heading as well as under the
headings shown. SEARS refers to the *Sears List of Subject Headings,* RG
to the *Readers' Guide to Periodical Literature,* NYT to the *New York
Times Index,* PAIS to the *Public Affairs Information Service,* and BPI to
the *Business Periodical Index.*

**Newspaper Indexes**  Newspaper indexes are a particularly helpful
source of information about current events and other newsworthy materials that may never appear in other kinds of periodicals. Such indexes
are published by *The Times* (of London), the *New York Times,* the
*Christian Science Monitor,* and the *Wall Street Journal.* The last is of
special help if your research concerns some phase of business.

### Using Periodical Indexes

In the front of each issue of a periodical index, you will find a list
of the periodicals represented in that publication, a key to the abbreviations used for their titles, and other information about the entries.

When reading entries in periodical indexes, bear these general facts in mind:

1.  Subjects are divided and titled in as many categories as seem necessary to locate information easily. You may want to look under several headings to locate all the material on a single subject.

2.  Titles are neither enclosed within quotation marks nor italicized, and only the first word is capitalized. Remember, however, that when *you* write the title of an article, it is enclosed within quotation marks and the first letter of each principal word (that is, all words except articles, prepositions, and conjunctions) is capitalized.

3.  After the title (and author's name, if it is given) there may be notations indicating that the piece is abridged, condensed, illustrated, revised, or that it includes maps or diagrams. All this, and other kinds of information, including the periodical title, is abbreviated.

4.  The volume number of the periodical is followed by a colon and then the pages on which the article appears. A plus sign (+) means that the article is not on consecutive pages but is continued elsewhere in the issue.

5.  Publication date is shown last.

## Bibliographies

Sometimes you can find additional source listings or save yourself going back through multiple volumes of an index by looking at appropriate bibliographies. These books are issued or updated so that recent publications on a specific subject (or in a particular publication) are readily available. For instance, the *Bibliographic Index* lists, by subject, bibliographies containing at least fifty citations to works that have been published separately or that have appeared as parts of books, pamphlets, and periodicals. Figure 13 shows a sample entry on "Hygiene." Note the "See also" listing and the "See" notation that lead you to other pages within the index.

**HYGIENE**
Abstracts on hygiene. Bur. of hygiene & tropical diseases. See numbers

Hockey, Robert V. Physical fitness; the pathway to healthful living. 2d ed Mosby '73 incl bibliog

Johns, Edward B. and others. Health for effective living; a basic health educ. bk. for college students and the consumer public. 6th ed McGraw '75 incl bibliog

Leaf, Alexander. Youth in old age. McGraw '75 p215-25

Murray, Ruth, and Zentner, Judith. Nursing assessment and health promotion through the life span. Prentice-Hall '75 incl bibliog

New Zealand. Education department. Health resource list; a bibliog. to accompany Health: suggestions for health educ. in primary schools. The department '69 32p

Schifferes, Justus Julius, and Peterson, Louis J. Healthier living highlights; health educ/health science text in personal and community health. 2d ed Wiley '75 p268-80

Woods, Ralph Louis. Government guides to health and nutrition; with commentaries. Pyramid bks. '75 127p
*See also*
Diet
Food
Health attitudes
Infants—Care and hygiene
Mental health
Physical education and training
Physiology
Public health
School hygiene
Woman—Health and hygiene

**Study and teaching**
*See* Health education
**HYGIENE, Industrial**
CIS abstracts. Int. occupational safety & health information centre, Int. labor off. See numbers

Canada. Department of labour. Accident prevention and compensation branch. Occupational safety and health; a bibliography. Sécurité et hygiène professionelles; bibliog [prep. by Celia Bookman] The branch '74 139p

Nesswetha, Wilhelm. Beanspruchung und Aktivation der Persönlichkeit; exper. Untersuchungen zur Frage einer neuen Arbeitstheorie. (Arbeitsmedizin, Sozialmedizin, Arbeitshygiene. Schriftenreihe, v30) Gentner '69 p90-104

Occupational health and industrial medicine. Excerpta medica foundation. See numbers

Peck, Theodore P. Occupational safety and health; a guide to information sources. (Management information guide, 28) Gale res. '74 261p

**HYGIENE, Public.** See Public health
**HYGIENE of housing.** See Housing

Fig. 13  Sample of an entry from the *Bibliographic Index: A Cumulative Bibliography of Bibliographies.* (Copyright © 1975, 1976 by The H. W. Wilson Company. Material reproduced by permission of the publisher.)

## Additional Sources of Information

Although the library is your best source for locating information, do not limit your search to the card catalog, periodical indexes, and special bibliographies. The list in Appendix A, beginning on page 135, will give you an idea of the many additional sources of information available in libraries. Note that besides general reference works, encyclopedias, biographical dictionaries, and so on, there are hundreds of works in special fields of study. (Obviously, only a selected list is printed here.)

Both in the library and out of it you will find other sources of information.

**More Library Sources**     (1) The *Vertical File Index* in a library lists materials that cannot be classified as either books or periodicals. These include pamphlets, booklets, clippings, and other useful items.

(2)  *Audiovisual materials* owned by a school or public library may be listed separately or with the general catalog. Such materials include recordings, films, slides, maps, and so on. They are a potentially rich source of research information. You could, for example, use a newsreel film or a taped lecture by a famous person as a source of information. In fact, if your subject for research is a film (such as *The Misfits* with Clark Gable and Marilyn Monroe) or the work of a director (such as John Huston, who directed that film), a film would be a primary source of information.

(3)  *Microfilm and microfiche* are being used to store a multitude of documents, from a single letter to an entire book. Many libraries have extensive microfilm and microfiche holdings; they are cataloged either separately or with other holdings. For instance, back issues of newspapers are usually available in this space-saving form, and a record of the periodical holdings of a library will show which issues it has. It is possible, too, to send for microfiche copies of works, such as the unpublished materials cataloged by the federally funded ERIC (Educational Resources Information Center) that are particularly valuable to education students and are listed in appropriate bibliographies. Obviously, there are many materials available on any subject, and these relatively new storage facilities, microfilm and microfiche, help make them readily available.

(4)  *Interlibrary Loan,* subscribed to by most libraries, enables you to receive and use materials held by another library. If you need a book not available in your library, your librarian may be able to borrow it from some collection in another school or city. If you decide to use the services of the Interlibrary Loan, allow for the fact that it may take a month or more before the material you request arrives and plan your work accordingly.

(5)  *Specialized library collections* may be good sources of information for your research subject. Many cities have museums or historical, legal, medical, engineering, or other specialized societies that maintain research libraries for their members. These collections can supply much

special information not available elsewhere. Try to use these additional facilities whenever you can, even if you need special permission from the holder of the collection to do so.

**Sources Outside the Library**    (1) *Interviews* can be a good source of information—whether the person you consult is an expert in the field or you simply need some kind of personal response from individuals. For a paper about safety innovations in passenger planes, for instance, interviewing an airline pilot or an aeronautical engineer will give you insight into the subject that no reading can provide. Such added knowledge and firsthand information will also enhance the originality and meaning of your research paper.

Before you interview anyone, be sure you are sufficiently familiar with your topic to ask intelligent and useful questions. Prepare at least the key questions in advance and be sure you control the interview in such a way that you get responses to the questions most important to your needs. Also, be sure you record both questions and answers accurately. A tape recording (if permitted by the person being interviewed), later transcribed, is excellent, especially if you wish to use a direct quotation. Highly detailed notes will not be as accurate as a tape, but they may serve the purpose. You should also know that many experienced interviewers use both notes *and* a tape recording.

(2)    *A questionnaire* that you prepare, administer, and evaluate is another form of original (and primary) research you may wish to use. You should know, however, that much of the value of a questionnaire depends on carefully framed questions and on the people you select to answer the questions. A questionnaire may prove a difficult and time-consuming method of gathering material, but consider using one if you think it will be helpful to your research and to the paper you will write.

(3)    *Letters* are another source of information you should not overlook. They are like written-down interviews and are therefore very useful in preparing a research paper. Write a brief letter containing specific questions directly to those people you feel can give you the information you want. Be sure to allow enough time for an exchange of correspondence before you need to write your paper, for you will not always receive an instantaneous response.

(4)    *Radio and television programs* are potentially useful sources of information. If you see or hear something of special value, write to the broadcasting station or network. Often you will be able to obtain a film, videotape or audiotape of the material; sometimes a script of the program is available.

(5)    *Reports, pamphlets, and booklets* may be helpful, so find out what is available or use your ingenuity to procure what seems potentially helpful. Private corporations, local, state, or national government agen-

cies and various social, business, and professional organizations print reams of material that can provide you with information on many subjects. The U.S. Government Printing Office also has available a wide variety of publications, many of them free, many of them not in libraries. Do not hesitate to write for materials that may be useful or informative. Some sources you can figure out for yourself (a request to the Airline Pilots Association or the Ford Motor Company, if you are researching aspects of safety, will certainly elicit the material each organization has available for public use) ; others you will find as a result of reading or listening ("Send today for your free copy of . . .") .

## The Preliminary Bibliography

So far, this chapter has been about places where you can find information on the subject you have chosen for research. Obviously, looking in each of these places is not enough: you also need to record the results of the search in some way. That recording of each likely looking resource (3 x 5 cards will be large enough for this) is the preliminary bibliography. It is preliminary because you may or may not use a source listed. For example, suppose you find in the card catalog the title of a book that seems potentially helpful. You would note the information about that source, including the library call number or letter on a preliminary bibliography card. However, after getting the book and looking through it, you might find that it contains no information readily applicable to your specific subject. You would, therefore, set aside the preliminary bibliography card for that book and not refer to it again—at least, not for this particular paper.

Because of the nature of the preliminary bibliography, you will obviously have many more items in it than you will in the final bibliography of your research paper. In addition to the case illustrated above, you may find that a book, apparently promising, contains essentially the same material as one you have already consulted. Or you may find that magazine articles you would like to consult, and for which you have made bibliography cards, are not available in either your school or community library; again, cards will have to be set aside.

You will have to use your judgment about which titles and descriptions of contents seem to be potentially useful to your research. Be cognizant of dates, for the time a book or article was written may turn out to be important to your work—ideas become less popular, additional study leads to new theories, and so on.

The preliminary bibliography is merely a listing; you should not look for or read the materials at this point but only note the possibilities.

## Uses of the Preliminary Bibliography

The main reason for making preliminary bibliography cards is so that you can have, readily and conveniently together, all the information you need to locate the research materials for your paper. You will have all the pertinent details and will not need to consult the indexes, catalogs, and so on again.

A second reason for making the preliminary bibliography cards at this early stage of research is to guide you in deciding whether you will be able to do adequate research on the subject you have chosen. Should you discover that you have no preliminary bibliography cards from periodicals (that is, that no periodical material was available on your subject), and your instructor has specified that you must use both books and periodicals for your research, you will know immediately that you must either abandon your proposed subject or confer with your instructor about the impossibility of following this requirement. Or, suppose your diligent search for research material leads you to only three or four very short magazine articles on a subject selected, yet your assignment calls for a 2,500-word paper; you will know immediately that your topic needs to be revised so you can find enough information to write from.

Still another reason for making a preliminary bibliography is to find out if your chosen subject is too broad for your purposes. A stack of forty-five cards gathered readily for a 2,500-word paper—that is, you found forty-five separate places containing information—means you probably ought to narrow your subject still further before proceeding with your research.

Finally, you will use the cards assembled for this preliminary bibliography to write your final bibliography. The information on them will enable you to document the text of your research paper accurately and without repeating searches you have already made.

## Preliminary Bibliography Forms

Remember that the preliminary bibliography gives you a record of all the sources of information available for research. Therefore, each card you write needs to be as complete as possible.

Use standard bibliographic form (described in detail in Appendix

B) on the preliminary bibliography cards. Accustom yourself to following such conventions as underlining book titles and putting the titles of articles in quotation marks. If you know that your instructor will require an annotated bibliography (described on page 132), leave room on the preliminary bibliography cards for notes from which you can write the annotation. (The two lines enclosed in brackets on the sample card in Figure 14 are the basis for annotation.)

On bibliography cards for **books,** record the full name of the author, the title of the book (underlined), the place and year of publication, and the name of the publisher. You may also find it helpful to make a note of any maps or other illustrations your source contains. In the upper left corner of the card, write the call number or letter of the book so you can locate it when you are ready to begin reading. You will get all the information for the cards in the library card catalog; the preliminary bibliography card will look much like a handwritten catalog card (see Figure 14).

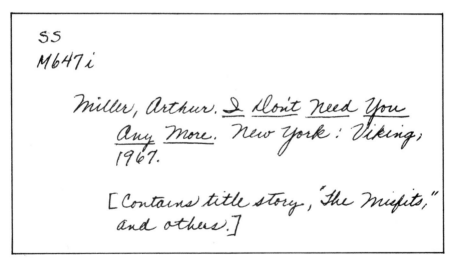

Fig. 14    Bibliography card for a book (with information for annotation).

Be complete and accurate when you record information about **periodicals** on a preliminary bibliography card (see Figure 15). Enclose the titles of articles in quotation marks even if they are not shown this way in the index. If no author is named, note this fact on your card and save yourself from having to check back later. Be sure to record the volume and page numbers or the publication date for all periodicals. You may also wish to note if maps or illustrations are part of an article. Sometimes it is also helpful to show the heading or subdivision under which an article appeared and the periodical index from which you got the entry. (See Appendix B for bibliography forms, including punctuation, for periodicals of many kinds.)

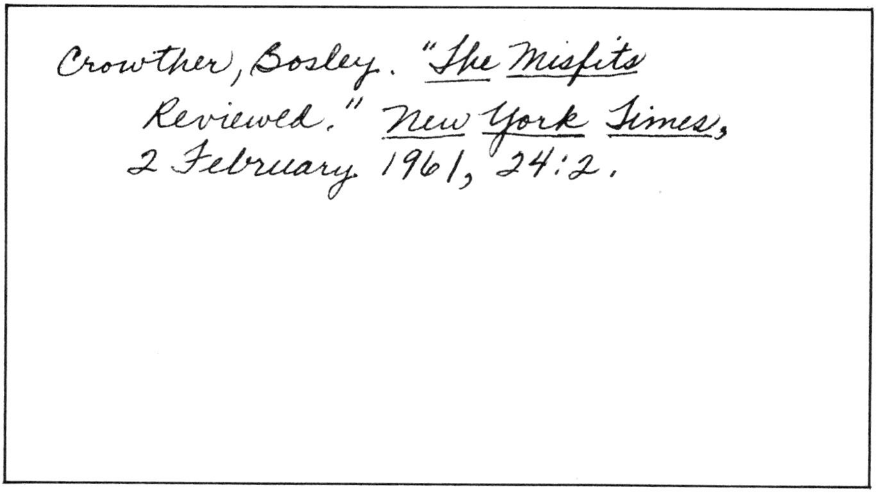
Crowther, Bosley. "The Misfits Reviewed." New York Times, 2 February 1961, 24:2.

Fig. 15 Example of a bibliography card for a periodical article.

When you check an **encyclopedia** article, record all the details about it that you will need in the bibliography (see Figure 16). If an article is signed, put the author's name on the bibliography card. If only the author's initials appear at the end of an article, consult the appropriate place in the encyclopedia for the full name; then record it.

Publication place is usually omitted. Volume and page number may be omitted from alphabetically arranged works. (See Appendix B for acceptable bibliography forms.)

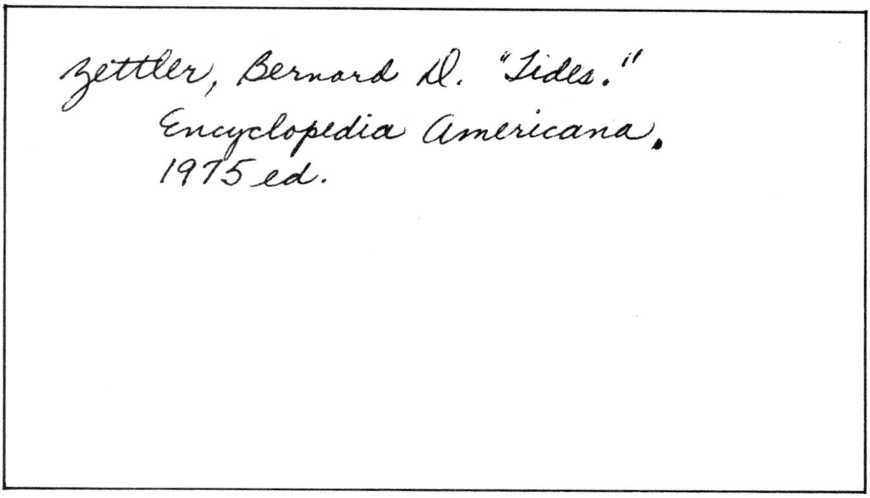

Zettler, Bernard D. "Tides."
Encyclopedia Americana,
1975 ed.

Fig. 16   Example of a bibliography card for an encyclopedia.

Pamphlets, videotapes, records, and so on that are found in the first search for information also need to be entered in the preliminary bibliography. Write a separate card for each item. As additional information sources such as interviews, letters, or an unexpected TV program develop, you should make a bibliography card for each.

# 5
## Recording Information

Begin your search for information by becoming familiar with your subject. If you are writing about a literary, dramatic, or philosophical work, or if your paper will be built around any other primary source, read or investigate that work first. Do not take detailed or extensive notes until you have some familiarity with your topic, for only then will you be able to be selective enough to take effective notes.

In addition to primary sources, you should try to get an overview of your subject. Consulting an encyclopedia or other general reference work is helpful. Then, from the sources recorded on the preliminary bibliography cards, select a few books and articles that, from the titles, seem to give general coverage to your subject. Look over those materials to get a feel for your subject. Read the table of contents of books to see how material is organized. Look through book indexes to discover the specifics that might be included in the subject. Many periodical articles and pamphlets have headings and subheadings that reveal their contents and organization. Skim sections of books and pamphlets that seem particularly relevant to your search and skim articles that appear to be promising sources of information.

## Evaluating Source Materials

One of the benefits of doing a research paper, as you have already read in Chapter 1, is that it helps you develop critical judgment. A good place to begin exercising that judgment is in reading your research materials and deciding which are most helpful and reliable. In daily life, as you already know, you cannot give equal credence to everything you read or everyone you hear. For instance, if you missed getting a class assignment, it is better to find out what it is from a good student than from a weak student who is often absent. Also, someone seeking to advance a particular cause is less likely to be objective about it than someone not immediately involved. Although judgments you must make about research materials are not always easy, the principles upon which they are based are similar to those you use for other choices. The following are some questions that will serve as guides to evaluating the materials you consult (and to making annotations [see p. 132] on your bibliography cards).

(1)  *Which authors seem outstanding in the field?* The names of some people may seem to recur as you gather information, and it is a safe assumption that those people are probably experts in the field and thus reliable sources of information. For while quantity of publication is not an infallible guide to a person's reliability, it is a helpful one.

An author's credentials may also be a useful guide to his or her standing in a field. An article on merchandising by a store executive or one on Mars soil experiments by a NASA geologist is likely to be authoritative. If an author is not identified in some way within the publication, you may be able to learn about the person by checking a biographical reference book such as *Who's Who in America* or *Contemporary Authors*.

(2)  *What is the date of publication?* While all that is new is not necessarily better, more recent materials often summarize or are based on earlier works. Reading materials in their order of publication may help you to see a development of ideas. Also, some scientific and technical fields change so quickly that recent dating of material may be a prime consideration for your research study. Or, a research subject may depend on reaction to a book at the time it was published or to an event when it took place. Keep in mind that many materials are written far in advance of the publication date shown. It may be a year after an author has completed a manuscript before a book sees print; many articles, especially those in scholarly journals, may have been submitted for publication more than a year before they appear.

(3)  *How credible does a source seem?* If your resource is a book, you can find out from reviews (*Book Review Digest* is helpful to consult) how it was received by critics. If the publisher is well known, the work might be more credible than if it were privately printed. Any bias you know a publisher has might indicate a similar bias in the material published. For instance, an article in a magazine published by a particular religious denomination would probably reflect the theological attitudes of that denomination. The extent of the documentation an author provides to support statements is another measure of a source's credibility. So is the author's use of mostly primary rather than secondary sources. The completeness of material in the introduction, preface, index, and

bibliography are further evidence of scholarship and, therefore, of credibility in a source.

If your resource is a person, make sure it is someone qualified to give you the information you are looking for. Asking a friend about weather on a particular date is less reliable than checking weather bureau records for that day. You may get opinions about the effect of a piece of state legislation from interviewing shoppers on a downtown street, but you will get opinions based on facts gathered about it if you interview state legislators who voted for *and* against it.

(4)    *What does the language of a source tell you?* The audience addressed, whether specialized or lay, is a clue to the kind of material you encounter. Language that is obviously slanted might affect your use of material—or the use you want to make of it. Discovering bias in a work does not mean that you must distrust the source or not use it; it simply means that you should be aware of the bias when using the source or when making judgments about it.

(5)    *Which sources seem to give you the most information?* Some reference materials will tell you more than others about what you are looking for. Also, some are especially provocative. Others are valuable because they suggest additional sources to consult.

(6)    *What facts keep reappearing in your reading?* If information is repeated in several sources, it is probably important; if something that seems standard is omitted, perhaps the source that omits it is not as reliable as others.

## Taking Notes

Once you have an overview of your subject and have looked through the specific items listed on your preliminary bibliography cards to make some judgment about their usefulness and value to you as information sources, you are ready to read the individual works closely enough to take notes on them.

There are three basic kinds of notes: **direct quotation, summary,** and **paraphrase.** A single notecard may contain just one of these types or a combination such as a summary and quotation.

### Direct Quotation

This is the easiest kind of note to take, but you should resist using it unless there is good reason. If you have many notecards with quotations, it is very tempting to use one quotation after another in the text of your research paper; instead of being an original piece of writing, then, the research paper becomes nothing but a cut-and-paste collection of other people's words. Direct quotations *are* useful as notes, however, especially in these three instances:

1.  The words of your source are written in a style so perfect, so suitable, or so vivid that they seem beyond changing.

2.  The material is so significant or controversial, or its source so authoritative that it must be stated with utmost accuracy. An example of all three of these possibilities might be an opinion written in support of a major Supreme Court decision.

3.  You want to be sure to record the exact words of a source. A notecard quoting a primary source will look like the one in Figure 17.

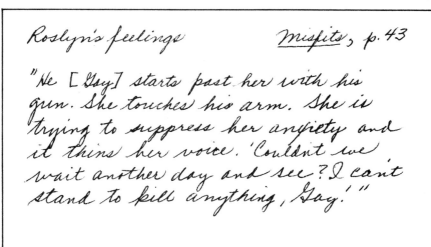

Fig. 17   Notecard showing quotation from a primary source.

Fig. 18   Notecard showing quotation from secondary source on the same
subject. [The slash mark indicates a page ending.]


## Summary

To record in your own words the essence of a passage and omit
examples, explanations, and other forms of elaboration is to write a
summary. A page in the original may become a paragraph in your notes,
and a paragraph may become a sentence or a few words. The summary
reports *only* what an author has *said,* not your interpretation or comment on the meaning.

For example, below is an actual passage from a book:

> As *The Misfits* flashes across the screen its images of the bedrock reality
> beneath the legend—the sterile glitter of Reno, the alkali wastes of the sur-
> rounding and encompassing countryside, and the shabby little towns that
> sprawl like mournful tumbleweeds across it—Biff's ideal is relegated forever
> to the junk heap of tarnished illusion. And certifying the death of the myth:
> the shoddy spectacle of the last of the rugged individualists—the American
> cowboy—hunting mangy horses with airplane, rifle, and rubber tires, to sell
> them for dog food because 'it's better'n wages.'[1]

[1] Benjamin Nelson, *Arthur Miller: Portrait of a Playwright* (New York: McKay,
1970) , p. 231.

A summary of the paragraph on a notecard might look like Figure 19.

*Symbolism*           *Nelson, p. 231*

*Reno, surrounding land, and local towns are seen as evidence of lost hope. So is the method of cowboys, apparently virile, hunting horses for dog food in an ignominious way.*

*summary*

Fig. 19   Notecard showing summary of a passage.

The word *summary* at the bottom will remind you which kind of note this represents.

### Paraphrase

This kind of note repeats phrase by phrase—but in your own words —what an author has written; therefore, the paraphrase is approximately the same length as the original. Paraphrase is useful in translating technical passages into lay language, and it is often used in exploring the meaning of poetry. Do not interpret the material in a paraphrase; just restate it. Figure 20 is a sample notecard paraphrasing the passage by Nelson shown above. The word *paraphrase* at the bottom is a reminder that this material is close to the original.

Nelson was writing about many of Miller's works. But note that the reference to Biff in the original passage is omitted in this and other sample notecards because he is a character in another of Arthur Miller's works and is therefore not relevant to the research paper on the development of Roslyn, a character in *The Misfits*, that appears in Appendix C.

symbolism — Nelson, p. 231

*The Misfits* shows Reno, the land, and little towns around it as they are in reality, not in story. The full impact of the dying "myth" of the west is the picture of supposedly virile and individualistic cowboys hunting run-down horses with an airplane, rifles, and old tires to sell them for dog food because they refuse to take work that pays regularly.

paraphrase

Fig. 20 Notecard showing paraphrase of a passage.

## Combination

Often you will find that the most effective kind of notetaking is some combination of the three basic forms of notes. A summary or paraphrase and a quotation is sometimes appropriate for notecards, especially if the quotation is brief. Or you might use a combination of summary and

symbolism — Nelson, p. 231

Nelson sees "the sterile glitter of Reno" and the emptiness of the land and towns around it as evidence of the "death of the myth" of the American west and the "reality beneath the legend." In particular, he notes "the shoddy spectacle of the last of the rugged individualists—the American cowboy—" reduced to hunting "mangy horses" for dog food because that's better than regular wages.

combination

Fig. 21 Notecard showing combination of quotation and summary of a passage.

paraphrase. The sample combination note in Figure 21 combines summary and quotation. The quoted phrases show this is a combination note-card, but you may wish to note that fact in the bottom right corner.

### Personal Comments, Ideas, Opinions

As you research your subject, thoughts will occur to you that have relevance to the paper you will soon be writing. There may be questions —and their answers—that you want to include. Surely you will have opinions about what you are reading. And you will undoubtedly have other comments and ideas as you read and think through the research material. Record all these thoughts on separate notecards rather than run the risk of losing what might be the most helpful part of your work (see Figure 22). Use the same form as on other notecards, including the

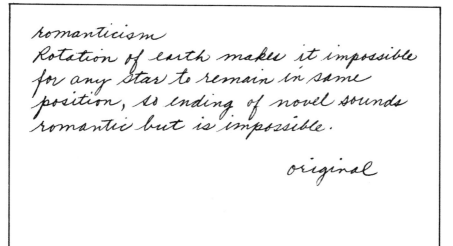

Fig. 22   Notecard illustrating personal comment.

identifying idea of each in the top left-hand corner. In the lower right corner write "original" to show that you are the source for the contents of that particular card. Then you won't worry later that you've not attributed a source accurately; you will know that *you* are the source.

## Unconscious Plagiarism

It is natural to want to catch just the right words on notecards in order to write the best possible research paper from them. Often the source from which you work has stated an idea so well you cannot imagine saying the same thing in any other way, and it is tempting to record those words but overlook giving credit to the original author. However, *plagiarism is using someone else's words or ideas without giving proper credit* to the person who devised them. And it is wrong to plagiarize, whether you do so deliberately or thoughtlessly.

An example of plagiarism on a notecard would be the combination example (Figure 21) *if* the quotation marks—showing that the original author's words were used—were omitted.

Plagiarism might occur on notes if the original material has not been adequately rephrased. Here is a passage from a book:

> Miller sums up the lonely, the searching, and the lost in Roslyn. But because he is drawing her, she is not all waif. Roslyn is the most pitiful of fanatics. She is gently drawn with an unmatched sensitivity; but together with the knowledge that she is fragile goes an awareness that she is also resilient. In her, you keep coming up against a totality, both of demand and involvement.[2]

Roslyn Huftel, p. 171

Arthur Miller summed up all lonely, searching, lost people in the character of Roslyn. He drew her as a waif and a pitiful fanatic. Miller drew her sensitively and with the knowledge that she is fragile but aware that she is also resilient. She is a totality of demand and involvement.

Fig. 23 Notecard illustrating plagiarized passage.

[2] Sheila Huftel, *Arthur Miller: The Burning Glass* (New York: Citadel Press, 1965), p. 171.

The example in Figure 23 is plagiarism because the material is not properly phrased in new words but is almost identical to the original passage —and does not give proper credit.

Avoiding plagiarism on notecards, whether unconscious or deliberate, is a good way to prevent plagiarism in the text of the research paper you write from the cards. Furthermore, if you clearly label the kind of note you have taken, there will be no question in your mind about whether or not you are close to committing plagiarism when you begin writing the paper. (See Chapters 1 and 8 for more on plagiarism.)

## Qualities of Good Notes

The notes you take will be used for the actual writing of your paper and should therefore be legible, accurate, and complete.

### Legibility

Several weeks or months may elapse between the time you take notes and the time you use them to write your research paper. Social events, other studies, all sorts of distractions will intervene. Therefore, you should be especially careful to take notes you can read and work from with ease at any time. Unreadable or garbled notes are worse than useless, and in redoing them you will waste time and effort. Here are some suggestions to help you prepare legible and useful notes:

(1) *Take notes on 4 x 6 cards* (unless your instructor specifies another size) . They are easy to handle and have enough room to accommodate most notes. Even if you have always prepared term papers from notes written on scraps of paper or in a spiral binder, start using the card method now. You will find that using cards makes it easy to arrange and rearrange your notes as you work until you achieve the most satisfactory order for your paper.

(2) *Take notes in ink.* Pencil writing may smudge or become difficult to read after much handling. If you can borrow library materials or use a typewriter in the library, you may prefer the permanence and legibility of typed notes.

(3) *Write on only one side of a card.* Use the reverse side only to finish a statement or complete a quotation. (Should you need to use additional cards for an especially long note, identify each card in the

series and fasten them together in order.) You will find that having notes written on one side of a card will facilitate arranging and rearranging the cards later.

(4)    *Put only one idea on a card.* Doing this will be helpful when the time comes for you to put the cards in order, preparatory to writing. An additional advantage of this practice is that you will not be tempted to combine different ideas which, although they come from the same source, are not closely related.

---

*symbols*                                     *Hogan, p. 38*

*desert location showing "wasteland" and half-finished house Guido abandoned that Roslyn and men use in* <u>*Misfits*</u>

---

*"outcasts"*                                  *Hogan, p. 38*

*Roslyn and three men in* <u>*Misfits*</u> *do not really fit into surroundings or form any real bond among themselves*

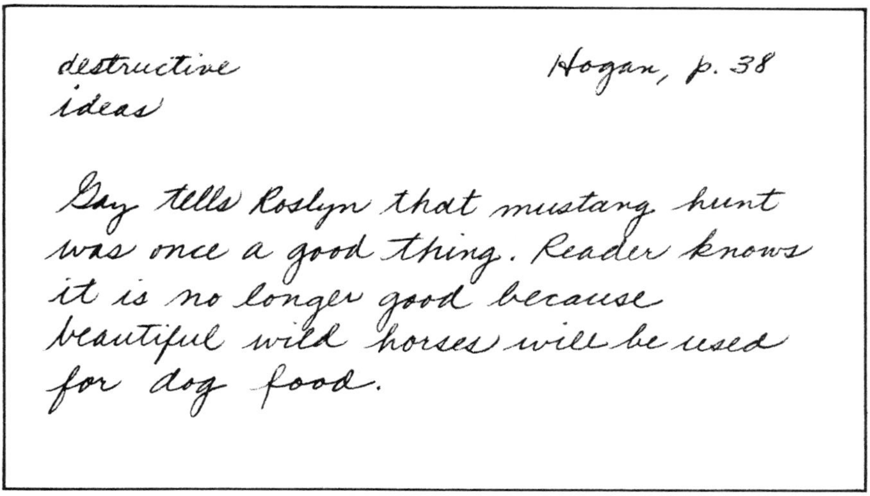

*destructive* *Hogan, p. 38*
*ideas*

*Gay tells Roslyn that mustang hunt was once a good thing. Reader knows it is no longer good because beautiful wild horses will be used for dog food.*

Fig. 24   Notecards showing different ideas from same source.

Figure 24 shows three notecards written for the sample research paper in Appendix C. Note that all three cards record material from the same page of the same source; yet because the three statements concern different aspects of the subject, each was put on a separate card.

(5)   *Use whatever abbreviations you find convenient for notes,* as long as they make sense to you all the time. Be consistent in the abbreviations you use in both labeling and recording information on the notecards. For example, if you use the letter *G* as a private abbreviation for "Goethe" one day, be sure you do not use it as an abbreviation for "God" on another day.

### Accuracy

When you are ready to write, you will have only your notes to work from. They must, therefore, reflect precisely the information you obtained from your sources. If the content of the notes is accurate, your paper will be accurate. If your notes accurately reflect what you learned from each source (and if they are accurate records of that learning) and if the notes are in a form that is easy to follow, they will be easy to work from.

(1)   *Read carefully.* Distortions, and therefore misrepresentations, result when material is misread. One word mistakenly substituted for

another can change the whole meaning of a passage and possibly of an entire portion of your paper.

(2) *Record precisely.* Carefully check the spelling of words in your notes against words in a text you are working from, especially if you are writing technical material or the words of the source are special or unfamiliar to you.

(3) *Distinguish between fact and opinion.* What you learn from a research source may be verifiable fact or it may be an opinion or inference drawn by the speaker or writer. Since it is unfair to let a reader of your research paper assume that an opinion is a fact (or vice versa), you should distinguish between the two when you take notes. A word or symbol on the notecard (to indicate whether information is fact or opinion) will easily prevent confusion when you write your paper.

Be sure to state, too, occasions when a notecard records *your own* opinion rather than that of a source you have consulted. Do not mislead your readers by making them think that an opinion or inference comes from published writing when it comes from you.

(4) *Follow the conventional mechanics of writing when you take notes.* Doing so will make it easy to follow them when you write the text of your research paper. The following are some conventional mechanics:

  a. Every quotation (that is, every excerpt taken word for word from the original written or spoken source) must be acknowledged—*both* by quotation marks *and* by notation of the source (see Figure 25).

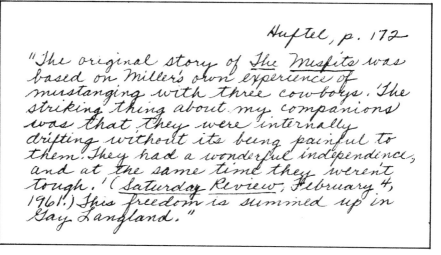

Fig. 25  Example of a direct quotation on notecard. Quote within a quote; original source cited.

b. Single quotation marks within double ones show a quotation within a quoted passage (see Figure 25).

c. Indicate omitted words from a quoted passage with the three spaced periods (. . .) that are called an ellipsis. In the interest of accuracy, you must use this signal to show that one or more words have been left out. Four spaced periods signal both an ellipsis *and* the end of a sentence. The ellipsis may be omitted at the beginning of a quotation that is part of a sentence because the lowercase letter signifies something is left out. If you want to omit a page or more between quoted passages, use a line of spaced periods to show you have done so.

d. Underline book titles, foreign words, and any italicized words in a source you are working from. Enclose the titles of articles and chapters in quotation marks.

e. Poetry of three lines or less is written in quotation marks in regular prose form but with a slash mark to indicate the end of each line: ''Busy old fool, unruly sun, / Why dost thou thus, / Through windows, and through curtains, call on us?'' Longer poetical passages are copied to preserve the typographical arrangement of the original.

f. Use square brackets to enclose an interpolation of your own within the text of a quotation. Some of the more common kinds of interpolations (1) relate a pronoun to its antecedent noun when the noun does not appear in the quoted passage; (2) enclose the word *sic* as evidence that the quotation is accurate even though something in it seems wrong; or (3) express a personal idea.

(1) The film suggests that she [Roslyn] got along well with the men.

(2) The soldier's letter to me said, ''Today we shot a bare [sic] near sundown.''

(3) An Indian's life expectancy is only 44 years [emphasis mine], almost twenty years less than a white person's.

g. Quotations within sentences are separated by a comma from words before the quotation; if the quotation is part of the main portion of the sentence, omit the comma:

```
Jones wrote, ''The women's liberation movement is
silly!''

Jones wrote that ''the women's liberation movement
is silly!'' because he did not agree with its
principles.
```

Observe the following punctuation at the end of quotations: Put periods and commas inside closing quotes. Semicolons and colons go outside closing quotes. Exclamation and question marks that are part of the quotation go inside the closing quotes; if they are part of the covering sentence, they go outside the closing quotes.

(5) *Information that is common knowledge does not need a source cited.* Certain kinds of information are so basic to a study or so well known that they need not be documented; this kind of information is called "common knowledge." For example, although you read in one particular book that standard sound movie film is commonly shot at twenty-four frames a second, or that Marilyn Monroe starred in the film *The Misfits,* you will certainly find the same information in many other places. Therefore, you can assume this information is common knowledge and that no documentation for the statement is needed in your research paper. Such facts as the date a literary work was published, the location of a famous battle, the chemical formula of a familiar substance, the birth dates of famous people—all are readily available from a variety of sources and require no documentation. You can safely assume information is common knowledge if it recurs without documentation in your research.

Certain value judgments may also be considered common knowledge and not require documentation. For instance, so many critics have said that Shakespeare's *Henry IV, Part I* is a better play than his *Henry VI, Part II* that you may consider this judgment common knowledge. (Of course, should you choose to use somebody's specific words for this statement, you would be quoting and therefore would need to follow the appropriate procedure.)

You may not always be sure whether a specific statement can properly be considered common knowledge or whether it requires documentation. In those cases, the safest rule is, "When in doubt, give credit."

## Completeness

If your notes are legible and accurate, they will probably also be as complete as they need to be. It is frustrating to discover, while you are writing a paper late at night, that important information is missing because you did not write it down or that you need to look at a source again to clarify some point. It is better to write down everything you think you might need and discard some of your notes or notecards than to find you must make another trip to the library or bother someone with a phone call because you did not take complete notes. (If you *should* have to recheck a library book, the call letter or number on the preliminary bibliography card will help you locate it quickly.) Here are several guides for making your notes complete:

(1) *Identify the source of what appears on each card.* The *top right-hand corner* is a convenient place to note that information because it can be seen easily. Use the name of the author alone if that person has not written more than one work in your preliminary bibliography. Use a book or article title, or an abbreviation of one if you consulted more than one work by the same author. If the date of a magazine or newspaper will be helpful, include that.

(2) *Note the page number from which you obtained information.* Putting that information on the *top right-hand corner* makes it easy to see, especially if you need to use the pages as documentation when you write the text of your research paper. Be sure to record all the page numbers from which you got specific information, even if you are summarizing a chapter or other long passage.

If you use a quotation that goes from one page to another, be sure you note on your card where one page ends and another begins so that you may be accurate in documenting the passage. A slash mark (such as that used to indicate the end of a line of poetry) is suitable for the purpose. (See sample notecard on page 71.)

(3) *Identify the subject of each card.* Use the *top left-hand corner* for this purpose. (See the sample notecards in this chapter.) These key words, or "slugs," will simplify the later work of organizing your notes because, instead of having to read through each notecard, you will be able to tell at a glance what each contains and arrange the cards in any desired order.

## A Note about Photocopying

With the installation of photocopy machines in libraries, a new way of recording information has opened. Instead of spending hours working in the library, it's now possible to make quick, inexpensive copies of needed research materials and work on them in other places and at other times. But photocopying book pages or even a complete magazine article is not a substitute for taking careful notes—not even if passages in the photocopy are underlined or otherwise marked for attention. There still remains the problem of having information readily at hand, in flexible and movable form, and often in summary or paraphrase. Only complete, accurate, and legible notes can solve that problem. So photocopy if you must, but use the material with discretion and work *from* it rather than with it.

## Number of Notecards

Students sometimes ask how many notecards they will need for their research papers. Nobody can answer that question. If you take effective notes, you will need fewer cards than if you record much extraneous material. If you already know something about the subject you are writing on, you will probably need fewer notes than if it is completely new to you. (Remember, though, to note the information you think you might want to use, citing yourself as source, so you don't forget anything important when you begin to arrange the notecards into order for writing.) Some students find that fifty notecards will suffice for a 2,500-word research paper; others need three or four times that many. It is the *quality* of notes that counts, not the quantity.

If you are ever in doubt about whether to record information or to ignore it, better write it down. Should you discover later that you have more information than you need, you can cut down the quantity. But once you begin writing your paper and discover you are short of material, you face a problem that is difficult to overcome.

You will probably know whether you have too much or too little information when you go on to the next step in preparing your research paper: organizing the material you have recorded.

## Reference Words and Abbreviations

Familiarity with words (and their abbreviations) often found in reference and scholarly materials will make your search for and recording of information easier. You may want to use many of them in your own notetaking and, later, in your own writing. There is a trend away from using foreign (mostly Latin) terms, but some popular ones are included in the following list.

| | |
|---|---|
| bibliog. | bibliography |
| biog. | biography |
| c or © | copyright |
| c. or ca. | *circa* ("about") —used with approximate dates |
| cf. | compare with |
| ch. or chap. | chapter |
| col., cols. | column (s) |
| comp. | compiled by, or compiler |
| ed., eds. | edited by, or editor (s) |
| e.g. | *exempli gratia* ("for example") |
| enl. | enlarged |
| esp. | especially |
| et al. | *et alii* ("and others") —always abbreviate, never use full form |
| etc. | *et cetera* ("and so forth") |
| f., ff. | following page (s) |
| fig., figs. | figure (s) |
| fn. | footnote |
| ibid. | *ibidem* ("in the same place") |
| i.e. | *id est* ("that is") |
| illus. | illustrated or illustrations |
| introd. | introduction |
| l., ll. | line (s) |
| ms, mss | manuscript (s) |
| N.B. | *note bene* ("mark well" or "take notice") |
| n.d. | no date of publication given |
| n.p. | no publisher given; no place of publication given |
| p., pp. | page (s) |
| passim | here and there throughout the work |
| pseud. | pseudonym |
| pub. | publisher, published, publication |
| sic | so, thus |
| tr., trans. | translator, translated by, or translation |
| v. or vide | see |
| viz. | *videlicet* ("namely") |
| vol., vols. | volume (s) |

# 6

# Organizing Ideas

A research paper is somewhat like an iceberg because what is immediately apparent is not the "whole story." Ordinarily, about 90 percent of an iceberg is under water and never seen by the unaided human eye; only people who know something about icebergs can fully comprehend and appreciate their immense size just by seeing that part which is above water. Similarly, an enormous part of the work of a research paper is not immediately evident to someone unfamiliar with the process of selecting a topic, locating and recording information, and organizing materials. What takes only fifteen minutes to read in its final form is the result of many hours of painstaking work that is fully understood and appreciated only by those familiar with the whole process.

When you finish taking notes, you will have completed an important phase in preparing your research paper. But it is only one portion of the task. Next comes what is probably the most challenging part of the process: evaluating the notes to select and organize the material that will finally be included in the paper. The ability to choose and interpret materials—and the willingness to discard what is irrelevant or repetitive —shows the critical judgment that is the mark of a good research writer. The process also helps you achieve that synthesis of your own ideas and your discoveries from various sources that is, by definition, a research paper.

You must do two kinds of evaluation at this point. The first is to study the bibliographic materials you used (not just the cards you have gathered for the preliminary bibliography, for you may not have found some of those materials helpful or even available) and be sure you have enough information. Check your bibliography now to be sure you have consulted a variety of sources and have not relied on encyclopedias or other general reference books. Be sure you have used primary sources (when possible) as well as secondary sources. Be sure the bibliography includes *both* books and periodicals—and articles from scholarly publications as well as from the popular press, if it is feasible. (Some subjects, such as a current congressional investigation or a local situation, will not appear in books, though background information might be found in them.) If you discover at this point that more research would be helpful, do it now.

When you are satisfied that you have an adequate bibliography and complete notes, you are ready for the second kind of evaluation: looking at the notes. That is, you need to decide what you can use in your paper and how each idea will fit into a general scheme. Allow plenty of time for this process and choose a large working surface (the floor or a big table is fine) so you can spread out the notecards, scan the contents of each, and arrange them in the most useful order.

The key words or slug lines will help you in this arranging, for they provide a ready-made way of grouping ideas. You will probably find that some cards can be shifted around and combined in groups with others. As you read through the cards, you may find you want to change some slug lines because ideas are related. Also, this period of reviewing notes is a good time to add cards expressing your own opinions.

As you go through your notes, you should keep in mind that you want your research paper to have certain characteristics, so choose the information you will use in order to demonstrate these. You will want your research paper to show that:

1.  *You understand the research process.* The thoroughness of your work will show that you have this understanding. So will the way you handle the content of the paper.

2.  *You have examined your subject thoroughly.* The ingenuity and energy you have used in gathering information will be evident. Thoroughness will also show in the details and support you have for the notes you include in your paper.

3.  *You have carefully weighed your information.* If you have selected sources with discrimination and then evaluated each notecard at this point in the research process, you will be sure of producing an authoritative and informative research paper.

4.  *You have taken a particular view of your subject.* That is, your paper will show that you have reached conclusions from research and that you are able to take a stand, make a value judgment, focus attention on something.

5.  *You have presented your material successfully.* The successful research paper presents and substantiates the point of view its author has decided upon and fulfills the requirements of what a research paper is, as pointed out on pages 7 and 8.

Those notecards that will help you achieve these five qualities are useful to you; others are not. Put aside, but do not throw away, any cards that do not fit into the scheme you are gradually developing. (Keep the cards not immediately useful, for you may decide to make changes later and will want the notes.) Disappointing as it is to omit cards representing hours of research work, you will be more disappointed if you weaken an entire paper by cramming in extraneous material or by making other poor choices in selecting material. (Make it a habit, too, never to throw any working materials away until you have received either a grade or some other indication that your work on the research paper is completed.)

The process of examining and evaluating your notecards will have three necessary results:

1. *The controlling idea will evolve.* This attitude you take toward your subject will help you develop a thesis statement for your paper.

2. *The emphasis you want to make in your paper will become evident.* When sifting through the ideas on your notecards, you will note a concentration of interest or importance on certain aspects of your subject; you will then be able to shape your material accordingly.

3. *You will discover an arrangement for your material.* Almost as a consequence of the first two, you will find that the information you have gathered lends itself to some sort of orderly or logical arrangement in which to present the content of your research paper.

## The Thesis Statement

The thesis statement is a specific declaration, a complete sentence that summarizes the point of view you will take in your paper or the propositions you will present. It states your theme or main idea and may range from one to several sentences, depending on the length of your paper.

One function of the thesis statement is to help you tie thoughts together and give unity to your paper as you begin to organize ideas; that's why the thesis statement is written first—before you begin final organizing of the material or writing. In fact, it is best to write the thesis statement *now,* so you can actually see the words on paper in front of you. A thesis statement in your head will not serve the same purpose as one on paper; it is too fleeting, too elusive; you need to put it in writing. You will probably also want to revise the phrasing a few times in order to crystallize your ideas and make them more precise.

Another function of the thesis statement is to assure coherence when you do further planning of the content of your research paper. If you have the written thesis statement before you as you work, you can check everything you write in the outline and the finished paper directly against it. Then, if you start to write anything that does not relate directly to the thesis statement, you will see the lapse immediately and omit what might interfere with the coherence of the paper.

Do not try to keep "stretching" the thesis statement—especially after you have formulated one that is suitable to the main idea of your paper; do not try to make it accommodate every phrase or idea that comes to you. By the time you have gathered and evaluated your material, you will have arrived at the principal idea that will govern your paper. Do not hesitate to discard information that does not fit with that principal idea. The organization, and therefore the effect, of your research paper will be weakened if you try to cram into it every single thing you have learned about your subject.

## What a Thesis Statement Is *NOT*

(1)   *A topic or subject by itself* cannot serve as a thesis statement. That information tells what the paper is about, but not what you have to say about the matter.

Subject:         New land for public parks
[Not a Thesis
Statement]

Capitalizing the first letter of each word would not make this a suitable thesis for a research paper, either, because it makes no statement. That is, there is nothing *said* about the land for parks. The phrase might make an acceptable title.

Title:         New Land for Public Parks
[Not a Thesis
Statement]

(2)   *A few words added to a title* but not forming a complete sentence cannot be a thesis statement.

**Not a Thesis Statement:**    What new land ought to be taken for public parks
and why

That is unsatisfactory wording because, although it suggests the contents of the paper, it fails to express an attitude toward the general subject or tell what the content of the paper will actually be. Moreover, it is not a sentence and is therefore not a complete thought.

**Thesis Statement:**    Citizens should work through governmental agencies to
set aside land for public use before business
interests destroy natural beauty and natural resources.

Now you can see clearly what the paper will be about. Furthermore, you can tell from this thesis statement something about the order in which the material is going to be presented. And the paper will be easy to write because the thesis statement has provided a framework which needs only development to express what you have discovered through research and what you believe about the topic.

(3)  *A question cannot serve* as a thesis statement because it is not a statement at all. A question only means that an answer will follow.

**Question: [Not a Thesis Statement]**    What are Leni Reifenstahl's contributions to film?

Obviously, the question does not set forth the content of the paper or suggest any framework for the presentation of information. An answer to that question suggests a thesis statement.

**Weak Thesis Statement:**    Leni Reifenstahl's methods gave new perspective to
filming sports.

The statement is weak because it is general. A reader would need to know what these methods were and perhaps what new perspective she gave to the filming. It is not a useful statement as the thesis for a research paper because it does not help the writer organize information to include in the paper.

**Improved Thesis Statement:**    Leni Reifenstahl's use of unconventional camera
angles and dramatic editing introduced an
artistic perspective to the filming of sporting
events.

With such a thesis statement, the writer can easily develop an outline that presents substantial information in a logical order.

# Methods of Organizing Content

Sometimes the organization of your information is dictated by the subject, but usually you must choose a way of presenting it. The most effective presentation follows a logical pattern that guides the reader to the same understanding of or belief about your material that you have already reached.

The thesis statement will often suggest a way of organizing your material. In the example of the thesis statement about citizens working to set aside land for public use, the content of the research paper might be organized in this way:

Problem:    Natural beauty and natural resources can be destroyed
            [by business interests]

Solution:   Citizens should work through governmental agencies
            now. They can do . . . [enumerate here what citizens
            can do to be sure land is set aside for public use]

The thesis statement about Leni Reifenstahl lends itself to this sort of organization:

One Cause:      Reifenstahl's unconventional camera angles

Another Cause:  Her dramatic editing

The Effect:     New artistic perspective to filming of sporting
                events

There is an element of time in the organization of the sample research paper in Appendix C because the two short stories upon which the character of Roslyn was based preceded the novel. The two characters in the stories are also "causes" that lead to the effect: Roslyn in the novel *The Misfits.*

Thesis
Statement of     Arthur Miller used elements of a sophisticated
Sample
Research Paper   mistress in one story and a childlike wife in

                 another to develop the appealing but not fully

                 explained character of Roslyn in the novel The

                 Misfits.

Here are some methods of organizing ideas for research papers—either used alone or, as in the case of the sample paper on *The Misfits,* overlapping or combined.

## Time

You can present material in chronological sequence. A paper explaining a manufacturing process, detailing the changing demography of a city, or the varying critical receptions of a novel over the years lend themselves to a presentation based on the passage of time.

## Known to Unknown or Simple to Complex

These two methods of organizing ideas are very much the same because they lead readers from what is familiar to what might not be known or understood. And what is simple or easy to comprehend needs to be presented before a reader can understand something complex based on the simpler elements. A paper on the Theater of the Absurd might begin with reference to more traditional or familiar theatrical types before progressing to the Absurd; a paper on the effects of prolonged space trips might begin by discussing the more familiar (and easier to understand) concepts of time as we know it rather than time as encountered on such trips.

## Comparison and Contrast

Both comparison and contrast show relationships between things, ideas, or people. Comparison shows similarity and contrast shows dissimilarity and, though the methods can be used separately, they are usually dealt with together when material for a research paper is organized.

One effective method of organization is point by point; that is, you deal with one aspect of the topic at a time, showing the comparison or contrast before you move on to another element of similarity or difference. Another method of organization is to write all the material about one subject before moving on to all the material about the other subject (and present all the material about each in the same order). Some examples of subjects that lend themselves to comparison and contrast are: an analysis of two different translations of a novel; a study of the employment programs of several candidates vying for the same elective office; a summary of the relative merits of three sites being considered for a new manufacturing plant.

## General to Particular or Particular to General

Material that follows the organizational pattern of general to particular begins with some fairly broad ideas or statements and then arranges the remainder of the information as a series of specific points in support. A paper might also be organized on the opposite basis; it could give specific points that lead to a general conclusion or statement. (There are, of course, specific and supporting points within any good piece of writing, but they are not the structural or organizational framework now being discussed.) A paper on the developing economic independence of African nations could begin with broad statements about how such independence was achieved; details of the experiences of several countries might follow. A paper on the short stories of James Agee might follow a particular-to-general organization: after several stories are examined, some conclusions about Agee's fiction could be presented.

## Problem to Solution or Question to Answer

The writer who states a problem that exists (or existed) and then either makes suggestions for its solution or shows how the problem was solved is using the problem-solution organization. For example, a paper about food distribution problems could first explain the situation and then present possible solutions to alleviate the problems. Many research papers on technical and business subjects use this organization.

Sometimes a question is posed and the paper is developed around an answer to it. The question would not, of course, be part of the thesis because there would be no thesis statement. Rather, the question would be, in effect, a problem to be solved. A paper might begin by asking how Mayan glyphs might be deciphered (the question: how can . . . ?) and develop by suggesting one or more methods not already tried. Or, the question might be about how it is possible to establish the authenticity of Shakespeare's work and the response might be an explanation of new developments in computer analysis to establish authenticity of writing styles.

## Cause to Effect or Effect to Cause

If you select either of these methods of organization, you will want to establish the idea of causality and maintain it throughout the paper. You could begin by writing about an event and then show its result. Or you could detail a situation and then trace its causes. Some topics that lend themselves to either of these two forms of organization are: how plastics have influenced industrial design, what Dostoevsky wrote about gambling and why he did so, or applications of the Taft-Hartley Act since it went into effect.

## Outlines

Once you determine the order of presenting research materials that support and amplify your thesis statement, you are ready to make an outline. An outline is simply an orderly plan, in writing, showing the division and arrangement of ideas. Its principal function is to indicate the relationship of these ideas to each other. You should not attempt to write the paper without an outline (even though your ideas seem well defined in advance) because only when you see before you the plan of the entire work can you judge the effectiveness of its organization. Furthermore, an outline enables you to see strengths and weaknesses in your paper and thus to make adjustments before you write. (Outlines put together after a paper is written just to fulfill an assignment are foolish and useless.)

An outline is to a completed research paper what a blueprint is to a completed house. The architect envisions a completed house but makes several sketches of its floor plan and elevation before being satisfied. When the blueprint is finally drawn, it shows exactly where the walls and doors, the plumbing, and the electric wiring will appear in the finished house.

So, too, by the time you have done research and are ready to write your paper, you know what you want to present. But because you may think of several methods of presentation, noting and rearranging the ideas on paper will help you reach a final decision. To help bring the many ideas of research into focus and proportion, some writers begin with a preliminary outline that may be no more than a listing of main topics to be covered. If the research paper is not going to be very long or will not contain particularly complex material, it's possible to do a first draft of writing from this initial sketching of the content. As with a painting, the subsequent details of the work—and a full outline—emerge from that sketch. The final outline will show where to put the key sentences, the paragraph breaks, the emphases, and the illustrations or examples that make a finished research paper.

The topic outline and the sentence outline are the two principal forms of outlining; and, since consistency is one key to successful out-lining, you should not mix the two. Choose one form and stick to it, using parallel (and consistent) grammatical structure.

The **topic outline** contains words, phrases, or dependent clauses fol-lowing the traditional outline symbols (see pp. 87–88). There is no end punctuation because there are no complete sentences.

The **sentence outline** presents statements in the form of grammati-cally complete sentences. In general, the sentence outline requires that you think through ideas more completely than a topic outline requires.

There is no way of telling how long an outline should be in rela-tion to the finished research paper. Since an outline is a guide, it should not be so minutely detailed that it becomes a paper in itself. On the other hand, it should not be so brief or vague that you need to guess about what is meant in order to join the notes together. Just as anyone can read a blueprint and have a pretty good idea of how the finished house will look, so anyone who reads an outline should be able to tell what the finished paper will contain. But the blueprint isn't the house, and an outline shouldn't be the paper, word for word.

## Outline Form

Outlining has several conventions regarding symbols, punctuation, and indentation that should be followed for the sake of clarity and con-sistency.

The symbols used in an outline show relationships among ideas and tell the reader which ideas are of equal importance, which are subordi-nate, and how all parts are related. Numbers and letters are used alter-nately. Roman numerals show the major divisions of the paper. The first subdivisions are indicated by capital letters; further dividing is by Arabic numerals and then by small letters. Further subdivision is pos-sible but seldom used for school research papers. If it is necessary, follow the number-letter sequence, first using Arabic numerals within paren-theses, then small letters within parentheses.

An outline shows the *division* of the ideas to be included in a paper, and since you cannot divide anything into just one part, numbers and letters in an outline must always appear at least in pairs: if you have an A, you must also have a B; if you have a 1, you must also have a 2; and so on. However, you may have *more* than two subdivisions. There is no need to make all subdivisions equal in quantity; your material and what you have to say about it are the only guides about how many sub-divisions should appear. For example, the following kind of division is perfectly valid:

```
I.
     A.
     B.
     C.
          1.
          2.
          3.
II.
     A.
     B.
          1.
          2.
                a.
                     (1)
                     (2)
                b.
```

Notice that every symbol in the example (except those enclosed in parentheses) is followed by a period. This custom should be observed whether you write a topic outline or a sentence outline. Also, in both forms, the first letter of the first word after every symbol is capitalized for consistency. Thereafter, capital letters are used only in normal fashion (titles, names, places, and so on).

Grammatically complete sentences require normal sentence punctuation, so there may be commas, colons, and semicolons, as well as end periods, in the sentence outline. The one punctuation mark you should *not* use is the question mark. An outline makes statements; it answers questions rather than asks them.

To emphasize the relationship of ideas and to make reading an outline easy, all symbols of the same kind should be in a vertical line on the paper. Roman numerals should be flush with the left-hand margin. After that, indent each successive symbol five spaces (if you are using a typewriter), or a multiple of five spaces, from the left margin: all capital letters indented five spaces, all Arabic numerals indented ten spaces, and so on. If you write an outline in longhand, use the same proportions for indentation; allow enough room to make the work readable and the relationships easy to follow.

If a statement requires more than one line, begin the second line under the first word of the preceding line rather than under the symbol.

```
A. This is an especially long statement and
   requires three lines; the subsequent lines
   begin under the first word above
```

The following page shows how to begin your outline.

Roslyn: Evolution of a Literary Character       Title centered
      at top of page

Thesis: Arthur Miller used elements of the       Thesis statement
      in sentence form

     sophisticated mistress . . .

I. Roslyn is an eastern sophisticate in ''The      Outline begins
   Misfits'' (1957)       here: single
      spacing permitted

Double-spacing the outline would be in accordance with the MLA prefer-ence for double spacing throughout a term paper. Some teachers may prefer single spacing. (Examples in the text of this book have been single-spaced; see the student paper in Appendix C for a double-spaced out-line.)

## Outline Content

An outline is meant to serve as a guide to writing, so every word in it should say something about the content of the paper to be written from it. For that reason, "Introduction," "Body," and "Conclusion" are words that do not belong in your outline; they only describe the divi-sions of *any* piece of writing (beginning, middle, and end) but give no information about the subject of your research paper. Instead of such unsuitable, catchall words, use language and information so specific that someone looking at the outline can tell exactly what your final paper will contain—including what will be stressed.

Suppose a portion of an outline about using videotape recording in classrooms looked like this:

Wrong:     I. Professional
          A. Who makes them
          B. Why used
      II. In-class taping
          A. Who makes them
          B. Why used

This is an improper outline because it shows very little information; certainly a reader can't discover anything the writer knows or has to say about videotaping in classrooms from looking at these notes. The "who" and "why" need to be specified.

Right:     I. Prepared professionally
          A. Sources
             1. Specialists within school

```
        2. Businesses and organizations
        3. Educational TV stations
     B. Advantages
        1. Variety of subject matter
        2. Professional production
        3. Money-saving
 II. Prepared in classrooms
     A. Camera operators
        1. Students
        2. School media specialists
     B. Advantages
        1. Immediacy
        2. Student involvement
```

Because an outline shows relationships among ideas, the *information for each subheading must be directly related to, and subordinate to, the heading under which it appears.* Since everything in the outline (and the written research paper) relates to the title and thesis statement, neither can appear as an individual item within the outline itself.

If you find that you have only one thing to say about any single part of your outline (and you cannot divide something into just one part), do not try to make artificial subdivisions. Instead, try revising either the wording or the idea of that part to eliminate the need for subordination. Here is an example showing how one section of the outline for the sample research paper in Appendix C evolved.

```
Wrong:  I. ''The Misfits'' appeared in 1957
           A. The story concerned three cowboys on a mustang
              hunt.
              1. Roslyn meets them.
           B. Roslyn is an eastern sophisticate.

Better: I. ''The Misfits'' appeared in 1957.
           A. Roslyn meets three cowboys going on a mustang
              hunt.
           B. Roslyn is an eastern sophisticate.
```

The second example is an improvement over the first: note that the single item is combined with what it initially seemed a part of and that the wording was changed to include the two ideas. However, it was still unsatisfactory to the woman who wrote the paper. She felt that since the subject of the research was Roslyn (the title of the paper is "Roslyn: Evolution of a Literary Character"), the focus of everything in the outline and paper ought to be Roslyn. Therefore, she changed the Roman numeral from the title of the story to something about Roslyn in that particular story. The final outline for the paper (you will see the whole outline on page 172) handles the material just described in this way:

Best:    I. Roslyn is an eastern sophisticate in ''The Misfits''
           (1957).
           A. She enjoys new sights and experiences.
           B. She feels sorry for hurt animals.
        II. Roslyn is a charming . . .

Reference to the three cowboys and their mustang hunt is omitted because the paper is about Roslyn, not them, and whatever needs to be said of the men will be worked into the content when the author writes from the outline.

Ideas of equal importance should always be identified by the same kind of symbol in order to make their relationship clear. That is, Roman numerals will precede all principal divisions of the paper's thesis, capital letters will precede ‚ideas immediately subordinate to the main divisions, and so on. Here is a sample outline of a paper about Ernest Hemingway showing headings that are not of equal importance:

Wrong:    I. Early journalistic career
         II. Participation in WW I
        III. The Sun Also Rises
             A. Other successful early novels
             B. A Farewell to Arms
         IV. Sympathetic to Loyalists
             A. For Whom the Bell Tolls
             B. Participation in Spanish Civil War

The phrases after each Roman numeral in this example give three different kinds of information: periods in Hemingway's life, a book he wrote, and an attitude he had. Assuming that (as I and II suggest) this paper is being developed around periods in Hemingway's life, III and IV are incorrect—their content differs from the others', they are not of equal importance in the outline.

Right:    I. Early journalistic career
         II. Participation in WW I
        III. Expatriate novelist days
             A. The Sun Also Rises
             B. A Farewell to Arms
         IV. Participation in Spanish Civil War

In the revised outline each symbol expresses ideas of equal importance: the Roman numerals show key periods in Hemingway's life, and capital letters show the two books that were written during one of these periods. Notice that the third book title in the original outline has been omitted from the revision because it would have had to stand alone. However, the writer of this paper may still say something about *For Whom the Bell Tolls* even without its being noted in the outline.

Parallel phrasing (that is, consistent use of the same grammatical forms) with comparable symbols will help you to write either a topic or a sentence outline without mixing the forms. Use full sentences, of course, if you write a sentence outline. Otherwise, you may use nouns alone, prepositional phrases, dependent clauses, infinitive phrases, and so on—as long as the same form follows comparable symbols (the Roman numerals, capital letters, and other symbols). The sample topic outlines on videotape and on Hemingway illustrate this similarity of phrasing, even to word repetition. The samples of the developing outline about Roslyn show how sentences make for consistency. Here is a part of the outline for the sample research paper (Appendix C) in sentence form (as it actually appears) and as it might be phrased in topic form:

**Sentence Outline**

I. Roslyn is an eastern so-
   phisticate in ''The Mis-
   fits'' (1957).
   A. She enjoys new sights
      and experiences.
   B. She feels sorry for
      hurt animals.
II. Roslyn is a charming,
    though essentially child-
    like figure in ''Please
    Don't Kill Anything''
    (1960).
    A. She is fascinated by
       any new experience.
    B. She cannot bear to see
       anything die.
    C. She is sufficiently
       strong-willed to ask
       something of the man.

**Topic Outline**

I. Eastern sophisticate in
   ''The Misfits'' (1957)
   A. Enjoys new sights and
      experiences
   B. Feels sorry for hurt
      animals
II. Charming but childlike
    figure in ''Please Don't
    Kill Anything'' (1960)
    A. Fascinated by new
       experiences
    B. Can't bear to see
       anything die
    C. Strong-willed enough
       to ask something of
       men

## Revising Outlines

Don't be satisfied with your first outline. Test it constantly, as you work, by thinking through each idea in relation to the others you want to express. Finally, when you think you have formulated a satisfactory outline, put it away and forget about it for a few days.

When you take the outline out again, try to put yourself in the position of someone who has never seen the outline before and is unfamiliar with its subject. Try to decide if that person could follow your ideas and understand your viewpoint on the basis of the outline. If that person can tell what your final paper will be about (but not word for word what it will say) by reading the outline, you have completed the necessary organization work.

Put your notecards into working order by keying each card at the top left corner to the outline symbol with which it corresponds. Then, should the cards become scrambled, you can easily put them again into the order you want to write from.

# 7
# Writing the Paper

If you have done fully and carefully all the preparatory work described so far, you will find that writing your paper is the easiest part of the entire research project. You will already have gathered all the material and know what you plan to say. Therefore, all you need to do is follow your outline and draw from your notecards to produce a good paper.

Methods of writing vary and you probably already have found one that is comfortable for you. Some people prefer to write slowly and carefully from the beginning, making corrections and changes as they go along. Others find the best way to write a first draft is to put everything down on paper quickly—in one sitting if possible—and then later make revisions, including the mechanics of spelling and punctuation. If you follow the latter method, concentrate on getting words onto paper even if you are dissatisfied with a particular passage; write yourself a note or use some symbol to indicate you want to pay special attention to that part when you begin revising.

## Writing Style

Research papers are usually written in the third person. That is, the words *I* and *you* will not normally appear in your text (though they may, of course, appear in quoted materials). By the time you have done the work preparatory to writing, you will be sufficiently familiar with the material to have a perspective towards it and will be able to write from the distance required by third person; that is, focus will be on the information rather than on the writer (first person) or the reader (second person).

Your research paper should be written in a straightforward style that is neither artificially formal nor as loose and relaxed as you would use for a personal letter. Many teachers feel that contractions are out of place in this style of writing. Thus, "Writers do not usually . . ." rather than "Writers don't usually . . ." might be the preferred phrasing. If you tend to write more informally than is suggested here, or if you have doubts about whether or not your instructor will permit contractions (and other such essentially informal elements), it is safer to ask the teacher's preference than to find you've used what is not permissible.

## Good Openings

The opening of your research paper should be easy to write because you will already have decided, and noted in the outline, what you want to say. You may begin with the first part of your outline or expand and develop a paragraph based on your thesis statement. Here are some ways to begin your research paper; each suggestion is illustrated by the beginning of a paper.

1. *Clarify the topic* you are going to write about.

It is not surprising that people find it difficult to accept the fact that they are dying. From the time a fatal disease is diagnosed until the time the patient dies, there are periods of denial of the inevitable. Patients will often talk about a mistake in diagnosis, discuss their illness as if it were minor, or make plans for the future. Through all this, the nurse plays an important role in helping the patient accept death.

*(from* "The Role of the Nurse in Relation to the Dying Patient" by Judy Blake)

2. *State your position* on the topic you have chosen.

Seldom do we have the chance to watch a dramatic character develop throughout various works by the same author. It is, therefore, a fascinating glimpse into the mind of playwright Arthur Miller to follow the growth of Roslyn. She is first apparent in the thoughts of the cowboys, Gay, Perce, and Guido in ''The Misfits,'' but does not actually appear in the story. Roslyn is unmistakable, however, in another short story, ''Please Don't Kill Anything,'' although she is not named but referred to as ''the girl.'' Miller finally combined the two characters for the Roslyn of The <u>Misfits,</u> which he called a cinema-novel because it used the perspective of film and its images, and was the basis of the screenplay he wrote for the film of the same name.

*(from* "Roslyn: "Evolution of a Literary Character" by Judith Matz)

3.   *Relate your topic to something current or well known.*

When Cortez and his small band of men finally reached the great city of Tenochtitlan on November 8, 1519, he was overwhelmed by the magnificence. The causeway connecting the mainland to the city was crowded with people, canoes came from all parts of the lake, and the temples were full of people. The Spaniards were met by Montezuma wearing rich clothing and carried on a litter with a feathered canopy decorated with gold and silver embroidery and a pearl and jade border. Two years later the Aztec fell, their empire destroyed, their people enslaved, their magnificent craft work almost entirely obliterated.

*(from* "Decorative Elements in Aztec Dress" by Gene Dynner)

4.   *Challenge some generally held assumption* about your topic.

People living in the public eye, particularly political leaders, always have a great deal written about them. If they are eminent leaders, their early lives and their most private moments become favorite topics for journalists. If they have been eminent leaders for a long time, so much has probably been written about them over a period of years that little,

if anything, can remain secret or hidden. Joseph Stalin
would seem to offer a perfect example of how the public
record reveals a man's private life. He ruled the Soviet
Union for so many years and was so constantly in the news
that it seems impossible for any facet of his life to remain
secret. Yet the truth is that few people really know anything
about Stalin's life. He himself undoubtedly destroyed most of
the records which might have shed some light on his true
personality and character. During his rule in the Soviet
Union, the history of his life underwent repeated revisions.
Since his death and subsequent ''disgrace'' so many other
changes occurred that the ''real'' Stalin may never be truly
known.

*(from* "Some Truths About Stalin" by Nancy Davis)

5. *Show something paradoxical* about your topic or about the material you will present.

Television is certainly one of the most influential
forces on society in this last half of the twentieth century.
Yet though it is called ''educational,'' it teaches little.
Though it is called ''real,'' it is fakery of the worst sort.
Though it is said to be a disseminator of American values,
it has worked to destroy them. It encourages violence,
passivity, complacency, and illiteracy simultaneously.

*(from* "Being There May Be the 'Great
American Novel' " by David Michaels)

6. *Use a brief quotation* if you can find an applicable one that is provocative or that makes a general statement about your topic.

''In an increasingly utilitarian age, one of film technology and 'participational media,' the word 'art' can seem
to have a narrow and effete ring to it. Yet to study the art
of the western in any depth, we must embrace both mass
culture and the individual film-maker, the industry and the

star, film history, American history, and film language.'''[1]
The western movie is indeed more than simple escapism,
more than wish fulfillment. It is a cinema genre with its
own archetypal patterns and a form so all-embracing that to
study it requires one to range over unsuspected areas.

*(from* "The Genre of the Western" by Sharon Lee)

7. *State some striking facts or statistics* you have discovered about your topic.

Only 53 percent of the voting-age population cast ballots
in the 1976 presidential election, a lower number than in any
year since 1948. Yet there were 79 million votes cast for
the two major party candidates, Ford and Carter, and the
incumbent, Ford, won 48 percent of them. That was just two
million fewer than went to challenger Carter. The wider
spread between the two was in electoral votes; Carter
garnered 272 of them and Ford only 235.

*(from* "Voter Apathy in National Elections" by Ciro Aldama)

8. *Give a brief description or background résumé of some person or event of significance to your topic.*

Lady Murasaki Shikibu was born about 978 AD and died
about 1030. She had the enviable position of being a member
of the Fujiwara clan and a member of a family which produced
Mikados, statesmen, and at least one celebrated Japanese
poet. Because she was of the nobility, she had the time and
the education to write. Her book <u>Genji</u> <u>Monogatori</u> (<u>The</u> <u>Tale</u>
<u>of</u> <u>Genji</u>) is the West's chief source of information about
court life in 11th century Japan.

*(from* "Amorality of 11th Century Japanese Life" by Margaret Haag)

[1]Jim Kitses, <u>Horizons</u> <u>West</u> (Bloomington, Indiana: Indiana
University Press, 1969), p. 175.

## Bad Openings

Just as there are good openings for your research paper, so there are also poor ones. These immediately detract from the quality that might be elsewhere in the paper. Some ways you should *not* begin the paper are listed below.

1. *Don't repeat the title;* it has already been read, and repeating it in the first paragraph is an obvious attempt to fill space.

2. *Don't tell explicitly what you propose to do in the paper;* the purpose should become evident without your stating it. "In this paper I am going to . . ." only puts off the reader and causes impatience. *Do* what you propose, rather than talk about it.

3. *Don't feel compelled to repeat the thesis statement completely in the opening of the paper.* Although you may certainly do so, you could also begin with the idea that is inherent in the thesis statement or you could vary the wording. Also, since the thesis statement gives the basis for your whole paper, it may contain more information than you want to disclose directly in the opening.

4. *Don't ask a question;* you may get an unexpected answer.

5. *Don't give a dictionary definition;* it gives the impression of dullness to come. You can probably define a term effectively in your own words. If you really feel it necessary to quote from a dictionary, at least wait until the second (or later) paragraph if you can.

6. *Don't write a cute or folksy opening;* it might fall flat and ruin the whole effect of your paper. Also, many people feel that a research paper is a serious work of scholarship and thus there is no no place for cuteness or excessive informality in it.

## Writing the Body of the Paper

Thorough research and a carefully prepared outline make writing the body of your paper easy. You will be explaining the thesis, using the material that supports it, and referring to the sources you have consulted. There is still time, during the writing, to summarize and paraphrase quotations you have on the notecards. That is, as you write, you may discover that a quotation you have put onto a notecard is necessary information, but that you can transmit it more effectively by another sort of reference. Do not hesitate to use that material in any suitable way—provided, of course, that you document the source and give adequate credit to the originator.

Allow enough time to explore your subject completely in the body of the paper. Remember that you will *not* be stringing together a series of quotations or paraphrases but doing original writing.

Take time when you write the paper to develop and explain ideas, just as you would in any other piece of writing. What seems perfectly obvious to you, after weeks of research, may be brand new to a reader and require explanation. Instead of simply mentioning a piece of information, you may need to give background or use an analogy to make it clear. When you use terms or names now familiar to you because of your research, you may need to define or identify them.

Support the statements you make, just as you would in any writing. Give details and provide examples if they will help clarify thoughts for the reader. Every sentence you can construct that backs up what you are saying in the paper is desirable because each makes a substantial case for what you have to say. If you express opinions within your research paper, be sure they have a sound basis. Adequate documentation will substantiate material obtained from your research sources and provide necessary support.

You will also want to observe all the traditions of good writing noted below.

## Unity

A unified paper is one that deals with a single idea. If you have chosen a subject carefully and prepared an appropriate outline, which you follow as you write, you will be certain your paper is unified.

## Coherence

The integration of ideas and details, the hanging together of a paper, is its coherence. It, too, is the result of a carefully constructed outline.

In a research paper coherence also means that the sources you cite as evidence are really necessary to the paper. If they are not, if they have been inserted only to look impressive or "academic," the paper is likely to lack coherence.

The usual transitional words ("therefore," "however," "because," and so on) help make a paper coherent because they pull ideas together. If you can blend quotations, references to "authorities," and statistics into the text, rather than inserting them as if they were afterthoughts, you will also have a truly coherent paper.

### Emphasis

Certain points in the text will need to be brought to the reader's special attention. You can do this either by proportion (the amount of space devoted to an idea) or by repetition of important aspects of the subject (or by both). You will already have decided in the outline to devote more space to some ideas than to others; by thus proportioning your material, you tell the reader which ideas you want to stress. You can also indicate emphasis by repetition of words and ideas in successive sentences or even at intervals in the paper.

### Consistency

Maintain the same writing style throughout your paper. Generally, a straightforward, informal style is most suitable for student research writing. Writing the first draft at one sitting helps many people maintain consistency because they get, and stay, in "the mood" of writing. If you cannot write your first draft all at once, reread what you wrote previously before you resume writing. Be sure to keep the same point of view throughout the paper.

### Clarity

The object of a research paper is to present ideas without confusion or misunderstanding. Therefore, you should write with clarity and leave nothing to the reader's imagination. Write down even what seems perfectly evident to you; your reader has not done the same research and will therefore not be as well informed as you are. Oversimplify if you have a suspicion that something is not being presented clearly enough.

### Conciseness

A concise paper is not necessarily a short paper, but it *is* one without padding; it is tightly constructed and has no wasted words. Say what you need to, develop and explain each idea sufficiently for clarity—and then stop.

### Concreteness

Specific writing is concrete, and the more concrete you can make the text of your research paper, the more believable you will make your thesis to the reader and the higher quality your writing will be. Concrete writing is also documented writing. The next chapter will give you information about how to document material you use in the paper in order to acknowledge your sources and avoid plagiarism.

## Good Endings

Stop writing when you finish what you have to say, when you come to the end of your outline and notecards. Of course, an abrupt ending is not good, and neither is a simple one-sentence summary of your paper; you will not want the conclusion of a good presentation to be sudden or awkward. The conclusion should reinforce your thesis, tie your paper together, and emphatically end it. Here are some suggested endings used by students in their research papers:

1. *Make some statement about your thesis* rather than merely restating it.

We have seen the Roslyn of the original story, whom the men wanted too much to please, become the charming but somewhat cloying girl of a later Miller story. When she was transformed into a major character in The Misfits, Roslyn grew in complexity and lost the simple definition of innocence or sophistication that each of her ''ancestors'' had. In these three works, Miller has provided us with an excellent view of the development of a dramatic character, from first sketches to boldly colored completeness.

*(from* "Roslyn: Evolution of a Literary Character" by Judith Matz)

2. *Use a brief quotation.* One that summarizes the ideas or attitudes you have expressed throughout the paper is appropriate.

Thucydides made mistakes, to be sure, but the historical significance of his work cannot be disputed. Like any great leader, he needed courage to break away from tradition and to introduce new ideas.

For he, as clearly as any tragedian, indeed as any Greek author, possessed the greatest of Greek abilities, the ability to observe the actualities of life with unflinching candor, yet at the same time, without falsifying these actualities, to reduce them to their generic and hence their lasting patterns. To have performed this feat both of record and of simplification on a plane of strict reality, and at a time when the basic political ideas of western man were at issue, is Thucydides' monumental triumph.[2]

*(from* "Thucydides as an Historian" by Gerald Douthit)

3. *Return to some initial generalization;* you may show how you have proved, disproved, or enlarged upon it.

Don Quixote, then, was not simply a mad old man. Rather, he was a person of deep humanity whose misadventures stemmed mainly from attempts to help the oppressed. Furthermore, what seem to be his foolish dreams are in reality the hopes of the sanest and least foolish of men; what seems to be his useless persistence is in reality idealism; what seems to be

[2]John H. Finley, Thucydides (Ann Arbor, Mich.: Ann Arbor Paperbacks, 1963), p. 325. [Reprinted by permission of the University of Michigan Press.]

his inability to cope with his time is in reality the doubt
and tension evident in the most normal of men. The character
Cervantes created cannot be called ''mad'' unless each of us
is willing to accept that label also. For he is a composite
of all—and each of us has within the self a bit of Don
Quixote.

(from "The Madman Who Was Most Sane" by Ida Kaufman)

4. *Link what you have written either to something known or to a future possibility* if both your subject and your treatment of it lend themselves to this type of ending.

When the Marquis de Sade published a novel in 19th
century France dealing with the raising and seduction of a
child, the public was outraged. This story, and others by
him, were so immoral, so heinous, that the poor Marquis gave
birth to a word which denotes all that is evil in man. Today,
and in 19th century France, the preceding acts [described in
other portions of the research paper] are considered immoral.
Yet in 11th century Japan they were evidently accepted as
part of a way of life. And it is evident that today, in
this country, as already noted, morality, like sanity, is
considered a relative factor which depends greatly on the
prevailing environmental influences.

(from "Amorality of 11th Century Japanese Life" by Margaret Haag)

## Bad Endings

A research paper is generally easier to end than to begin. Nevertheless, bad endings are written and an otherwise good paper can be weakened by a bad ending. To avoid such a possibility:

1.  Don't bring up a new idea; this is the end of the paper, and not a place to start anything new.

2.  Don't make any statement or suggestion that needs extensive clarification; the time to make explanations is past.

3.  Don't fumble; stop when you have nothing more to say.

## Revising the Paper

Professional writers are not usually satisfied with their first drafts. In fact, it has been said that writing should more aptly be called "rewriting." Revision gives you a chance to take another look—literally—at what you have done. Although thorough revision of a theme written under the pressure of time in class might involve radical rethinking, the revision of a research paper that has been thoroughly prepared does not involve anything as dramatic as tearing up the work and starting over again. Rather, after you have written a first draft of the paper you should check it over for good word choice and sentence structure, mechanics, smooth transitions, accuracy, and general good quality of writing.

Revision is made easier if you can look at your paper as if for the first time. It's a good idea to put away the first draft of your paper for several days—a week or more, if you can. Then, when you are ready to work again, read it over so you will be able to see the paper more objectively than when you were deeply involved in it. Try, also, to allow time for at least a second revision—again, after not looking at the work for a few days. You will find that each time you look at what you have written, you can make improvements. Additional changes can even be made during the final typing (or copying), for revision need not stop until your research work is turned in. The following are some aspects of your work that you should evaluate in revision.

### Word Choice and Sentence Structure

When people write ideas down on paper, they sometimes cannot find just the "right" word to state a particular idea. Instead of stopping and losing a train of thought, they either use a "second best" word or mark the word used in some way to show that improvement or restatement is needed. During revision, you can check for such wording that might need to be changed and improved. Take time to select the most appropriate words for every idea within the paper.

Sentence structure, too, can be improved in revision. Make sure that sentences are complete, that modifiers are near the words they modify, that the antecedents of pronouns are clear, and that each sentence says exactly what you intend it to say. Make sure that the words in your writing flow smoothly and freely so a reader can concentrate on what you say in your paper rather than getting bogged down trying to understand what you *mean* (but aren't saying).

## Mechanics

Readers usually expect to find the spelling, punctuation, and paragraphing associated with professionally written and edited text. It is, therefore, helpful to readers of your paper to follow the conventions expected. Make sure punctuation and capitalization are accurate. If you are in doubt about the spelling of any word, look in a dictionary to find conventional spelling; then use it. Be sure that tenses do not shift without reason and that subjects and verbs agree in number. Underline what needs to be emphasized or what would be italicized in print. Be sure abbreviations are accurate and are used only where permissible.

## Smooth Transitions

Transitions are connecting words or passages; they tie ideas together for a smooth flow. What began as a series of unrelated notes on cards has finally been combined in the writing of your paper. During revision you should be sure that those thoughts and references are really combined so the reader can follow with ease (and doesn't have to keep wondering why one thing is said but not another or how one idea relates to another).

Be sure, too, that quotations fit where they are used and are not put in as padding to make a paper look longer or more impressive than it really is. This integration of quotations and original writing is an important aspect of writing with clear transitions.

## Accuracy

A research paper demands that you present accurate material, so when you revise your paper, look up any facts about which you may be uncertain. Be sure quotations have been copied exactly as they appeared in your sources, and if you have any doubt, return to the original source and check. Finally, be certain that all documentation is presented in the prescribed forms.

### Quality of Writing

At the beginning of this chapter, you read about seven qualities of good writing: unity, coherence, emphasis, consistency, clarity, conciseness, and concreteness. As you revise, be sure that your paper has these qualities. Be sure, also, that you have neither contradicted yourself nor been repetitious.

After careful and thoughtful revision, you will be ready to type your research paper, add a title ( and other needed material such as an outline and bibliography) , and present it to your instructor.

## Selecting a Title

Your research paper will be known by its title, so it is important to choose carefully the one that will appear on the title page. A title that gives readers some information about the contents of the paper is preferable to one that is general or vague.

Vague:      Commercial Fishing
Improved:   Commercial Fishing Rights and Territorial Waters

Vague:      A Look at William Dean Howells
Improved:   The Concept of Work in the Novels of William Dean
            Howells

Vague:      Faust Legends
Improved:   Faust Viewed by Gounod and Goethe

Vague:      Auto Insurance Rates
Improved:   Legislative Influences on Auto Insurance Rates

The student who wrote the sample research paper in Appendix C planned, at one time, to use a descriptive title: ''The Character of Roslyn in Three Works by Arthur Miller.'' While working on the research materials, she decided to change the title because she saw the character developing and gaining dimension in the two stories and the cinema-novel. Ms. Matz then decided on the present title—`'Roslyn: Evolution of a Literary Character'`—because it conveyed the precise focus of her paper.

A title need not be stuffy or dull. However, it should not be "cute" —even if your subject is a humorous one. Puns and clever wordings are, of course, permissible. Do not use a question in place of a title, for no matter how provocative one might be, it won't be informative enough. Finally, do not use a thesis statement as a title, for it is bound to be too long and tell *too* much.

# 8

## Documentation

You help establish the veracity of your research paper and of your academic ability by *acknowledging and documenting COMPLETELY all material in the paper that is not original.* Specifically, three kinds of material require documentation (that is, acknowledgment of the source) in a research paper:

1. Direct quotations
2. Borrowed ideas, including paraphrases and summaries
3. Visual material such as maps, charts, diagrams, and pictures

Any idea or any words you got from a source other than yourself (or any not considered "common knowledge," as explained on page 72) needs to be acknowledged by documentation. Such recognition not only establishes your own honesty and scholarly exactness but also gives support to your ideas and conclusions. The acknowledgment also enables a reader to identify or to verify your material and, if desired, to study further any aspect of it.

The question of what needs documentation and what does not is sometimes troublesome. A general rule to follow is: when in doubt, cite the source. It is better to have too much documentation than too little.

Plagiarism—using somebody else's material as if it were your own (that is, without citation)—is less likely if you were cautious about acknowledgment when taking notes. But be aware that, unless you are alert while writing the paper, it is still possible to commit plagiarism.

### Direct Quotations

Using the words of another writer (or speaker, if you are working from audio sources) must be acknowledged *in two ways* within your research paper:

1.  Use quotation marks or set off the quoted lines (if there are four or more in the passage) by indentation

2.  Indicate the source in a footnote, an in-text citation, or a note page. (The following pages give details of the customary forms for citing sources.)

Whatever the *form* you use for setting off a quotation—and it will differ depending on whether the passage you quote is prose, poetry, or drama, or is long or short—you must *always* cite the source. Citations are numbered consecutively throughout the paper. Those in long papers and reports may be numbered by chapters or sections. In this book they are numbered by chapter; *examples* have been given numbers outside the normal sequence to help distinguish them from citations to this book.)

## Prose Quotations

Quotations of four lines or less are typed as part of the written text and are enclosed in quotation marks. *After the ending quotation mark,* and even with it (that is, a half space above the line), type in a number that identifies the quotation and is matched with the citation for that passage. An example from the sample research paper in Appendix C is:

```
They appear at first to be capable of little understanding.
''They are scatterbrained, whimsical, lonely . . . they are
amusing people to be with, for a little while, anyhow. But
they are shallow and inconsequential. . . .'''¹¹ Roslyn and
Gay become lovers, . . .
```

Longer passages would interfere with the flow of writing in a research paper. Therefore, if a quotation is more than four lines long, indent eight or ten spaces from the left margin of the text—enough to differentiate between the quotation and a standard paragraph indentation. Traditionally, such passages have been typed single-spaced, but a newer, more readable style (recommended by the MLA) is to maintain double spacing within quotations, and to triple-space before and after the quotation. Do *not* use quotation marks at the beginning or end of the passage;

---

¹¹Bosley Crowther, ''The <u>Misfits</u> Reviewed,'' <u>New York Times</u>, 2 February 1961, p. 24, col. 2.

the indentation is a signal that the lines are a quotation. Do not indent the beginning of the quotation (even if it is the start of a paragraph) unless you are quoting two or more paragraphs consecutively.

Echoing the bleak message, another critic finds:

> The <u>Misfits</u> is about death . . . on many levels:
> the death of a world—the West as it once was—and
> the death of a myth—the dream of the West as it
> never quite was; the death of human relationships
> and the destruction of personal values. On its
> most elemental level it is about the death of some
> misfit horses, which symbolize the figurative
> demise of some misfit people in a misfit world.[13]

If you submit a handwritten paper, follow the same general form and use comparable indentation to signal a long passage that is quoted.


### Poetry Quotations

Quoted poetry of three lines or less can be written as part of the text, but enclose the words in quotation marks, follow the author's punctuation and capitalization, and use a slash mark (/) to show the end of each line of poetry. For example, you could quote from Shakespeare's Sonnet 116 in this way: ''Let me not to the marriage of true minds / Admit impediments. Love is not love / Which alters when it alteration finds.'' If the citation were not otherwise identified (as it is here in the text immediately before the quotation), the citation number would be placed after the concluding quotation marks.

To quote longer passages of poetry, use the same form already recommended for quoting longer prose passages: double-space the lines (some teachers may prefer single spacing) and indent them at least eight or ten spaces from the left margin. Some teachers may prefer that quotations also be indented from the right margin. Do not use quotation marks. Triple-space before and after the quotation. Remember that accurate

---

[13]Nelson, p. 227. [That is how the citation actually appears in the research paper in Appendix C because the book from which this idea is taken has already been identified more completely in an earlier note.]

quotation of poetry requires that you reproduce the *original typography* —that is, copy indentations, capitalization, punctuation, and spelling *exactly as it appears in the original.*

If you quote a complete poem, you should identify the author and title in the text or at the beginning as in this example:

The Unknown Citizen

by W. H. Auden

If you quote a longer passage of a poem, put the citation number at the conclusion of the passage, just as you would in quoting prose. Be sure to identify the number of the lines quoted; count from the first typographical line of the beginning to the last lines you quote, such as (ll. 26–32).

### Dramatic Quotations

Follow the same form for quoting passages from plays as you would for quoting prose (or poetry, if the play is in poetic form). That is, a few lines can be incorporated into the text, but longer passages should be separately indented and typed double-spaced. Be sure to include the name of the character speaking the lines you quote and more than one name if the passage includes the speeches of more than one character. The citation identification number of each passage is put at the conclusion of the quotation.

## Punctuating Quotations

Wording that is not your own is acknowledged by being put in quotation marks and being properly acknowledged. A quotation *within* a quotation is shown by enclosing those words in single quotation marks. For example:

''On the subject of <u>human</u> life, however, her youthful

wonderment changes to adolescent precocity . . . even her

. . . most credible act, abounds in vague generalizations:

'Big man! You're only living when you can watch something

```
die!  .  .  .  You know everything except what it feels like to
be alive (p. 118).' Again she leaves the point unclear.''²¹
```

Commas and periods are placed within the quotation marks, and other punctuation, unless it is part of what is quoted, goes outside the quotation marks.

## Introducing Quoted Material

Quotations should be worked smoothly into the text of your paper so that the material does not interfere with the flow of ideas. The quoted material may follow a complete sentence related to it as shown and documented in the prose quotation on page 176 in Appendix C:

```
They appear at first to be capable of little under-
standing. ''They are scatterbrained, whimsical,
lonely. . . .''¹¹
```

Or, the quotation may come as the conclusion of a statement, as illustrated and documented in the same section on page 177.

```
Echoing the bleak message, another critic finds:
     The Misfits is about death . . . on many levels: the
     death of a world. . . .¹³
```

Note that the colon is used here to show that a long statement (or enumeration or lines of verse) is to follow.

A quotation may become part of a sentence, as it does in this example from the sample research paper in Appendix C.

```
     Gay, agreeing with Perce that Roslyn would have loved to
     have seen the antelope they spotted, thinks of her ''eastern
```

²¹Leonard Moss, Arthur Miller (New York: Twayne, 1967), p. 77. [The page number within the quotation in parentheses is Moss' own documentation.]
¹¹Bosley Crowther, ''The Misfits Reviewed,'' New York Times, 2 February 1961, p. 24, col. 2.
¹³Nelson, p. 227. [This is the actual citation used in the sample research paper because the source has already been identified completely. Read about Subsequent References beginning on page 119.]

```
surprise at everything they did and saw and said,''²  thus

giving us a glimpse of the wonder-filled Roslyn of the

future work.
```

In general, the more smoothly you can make a transition from original to quoted material, the better it is for the writing style of your paper and for the reading comfort of those who will see your work.


## Maps, Charts, Diagrams, Pictures

Many research papers are enhanced by including visuals—maps, charts, diagrams, or pictures. If these materials do not originate with you, they are quotations from a source, and, as with quoted words, their sources need to be acknowledged. Reproduce the visual exactly as you found it, either by drawing or photocopying the original, and include it in the appropriate place in your paper. Then credit the original source in a caption placed below the material.


## Borrowed Ideas

The source of any thought, opinion, or conclusion that appears in your paper but that did not originate with you needs to be acknowledged. If you summarize another person's ideas, even though the summary contains your own words, you should let your reader know that the thought is not your own. If you paraphrase anyone's material, you should let the reader know you are doing so. If you fail, either intentionally or through oversight, to acknowledge borrowed ideas, or summarized or paraphrased material (which should already be identified for what it is on your note-cards), you will be committing plagiarism.

A frequent question is "How 'original' must one be in order not to be required to supply documentation to recognize a source?" It is difficult to give a single, pat answer. On the most literal level probably nothing you write is completely original because everything you know had to be

²**Page 90.** [This is also a Subsequent Reference. See page 174 for this passage actually used in the sample research paper.]

learned from someone or something. The very words you use for writing the paper are certainly not "original" in the sense that they have never been used before by any person. Obviously, to take "originality" so rigidly would mean nobody could communicate. Likewise you cannot remember the source of every fact and idea you have, even those closely related to your research subject. So judgment must necessarily play a large part in determining what is rightly your own and what is not. However, a good rule to follow is: when in doubt, document.

Acknowledge by citation the source of a paraphrased idea; follow the same procedure you would for a quotation (except, of course, no quotation marks will appear in your written portion).

```
Roslyn's strong character is temporarily masked by her

femininity, but both characteristics are necessary to her

place in the lives of the three cowboys.⁸
```

Compare this borrowed idea, a paraphrase, with the original quotation from Nelson used on page 179 in the sample research paper in this book.

## Location of Documentation

The *MLA Handbook* recommends putting documenting citations at the end of the research paper on a sheet headed "Notes," and that is the style followed in the sample research paper in Appendix C. The familiar "footnotes" are, literally, notes at the "foot" or bottom of a page and some instructors prefer that location for ease of reading. It is becoming increasingly popular to place documentation within the text itself. There is also a style of documentation in which the note appears as an "interrupter" in the text, following as soon after the citation as possible.

### Endnotes

You can put all your documentation and commentary notations together on a separate page or pages at the end of the research paper text

⁸Benjamin Nelson, Arthur Miller: Portrait of a Playwright (New York: David McKay, 1970), p. 228. [Note that this example does not appear in the sample research paper.]

and immediately before the bibliography. Head the page "Notes" (since they are not really "footnotes"). Double-space all the entries. (Double spacing is preferred by the MLA; some teachers may prefer that you single-space entries of more than one line—as you would for footnotes—and double-space between entries.) You should use the same internal form for endnotes as you would for citations in any other location.

This form is easy for a typist, since there is no need to place material between the text and the bottom of the page, but it may be awkward for a reader because it means turning from text to notes and back again when all the pages of a research paper are fastened together.

## Footnotes

Footnotes appear on the bottom of the page on which a passage to be acknowledged appears (or where a comment is to be made). If you know you will have two footnote numbers in the text of one page, you will need to leave room for both when you type the final copy of your paper; if you have five footnote numbers on one page, you will have to leave room for all five citations. It takes some practice (or some line-by-line counting) to learn how much room to allow for footnotes when you are typing, but you will soon be able to judge the right amounts of space. Single-space the footnotes and double-space between them.

Separate the text and the first footnote by spacing four times. (Some teachers may prefer double spacing and a solid line extending at least one-third of the way—it may be all the way—across the page. If you use the line, skip a space between it and the notes.)

## Interlinear Notes

It is acceptable to present documentation immediately following the line on which an identifying number appears in the text, in this fashion:[1]

---

[1]This method makes it easy for the reader to find the citation. However, it requires drawing or typing many lines across the paper and if you have several items on a page to document, the style seems to interfere with the text.

---

This form customarily is double-spaced between the text and the top line. Another double space is used between the top line and the figure indicating the documentation, but only a single space between the last line of the citation and the lower line. You should then double-space before resuming the written text.

## In-Text Documentation

It is becoming increasingly popular to cite each source within the text to the extent that you can do so without breaking the continuity of your writing. For example, this passage appears on page 177 in the sample research paper.

. . . The Misfits, which The Times of London (30 May 1961,

p. 18) has found to be concerned with utter despair:

''Despair that modern life makes true virility—equated

with the frontier values of the man without ties who must

be his own master and for whom anything is better than wages

—impossible. Despair that whatever one's intentions life

makes a mockery of them and soils everything.''[12]

Another way the same citation might have been handled as in-text documentation would be to put the needed research information at the end of the quotation.

**Alternate**

This sketch of the story cannot convey the impact of The

Misfits which has been found to be concerned with utter

despair: ''Despair that modern life makes . . . a mockery of

them and soils everything'' (The Times of London, 30 May

1961, p. 18). Roslyn provides the only relief from this

hopelessness by demonstrating that the men can control their

lives.

There are other possibilities, for the method is flexible; any way can be used that is suitable to the free flow of words in text and can accommodate the citation.

[12]Quoted in Huftel, pp. 166—167

An in-text citation of a book might appear this way:

```
Early in The Grapes of Wrath (John Steinbeck. New York:
Compass Books, 1962, p. 48) there is this description of the
impersonal destruction of the farm by the tractors. . . .
```

Note that the name of the book is omitted because it is part of the intro-
ductory textual statement.


## Content of Notes


Most frequently, notes acknowledge material and credit sources used
in the text. They require the author and title of the work used, par-
ticulars about publication, and the exact page used (including column
number of newspapers) . The first three items you can get from the bibliography cards you have prepared; the last item will come from your notecards. The usual form of notes and footnotes from a variety of sources is
explained on pages 118–125 and examples appear in Appendix B on
pages 158–168.

Notes also offer a way for the author to comment on the content of a
paper without disrupting the flow of the text. Some of the kinds of comments that may conveniently be expressed in notes are:


1.  Elaboration, qualification, or additions to something just writ-
    ten. Put the documentation number at the conclusion of the idea
    that is being commented on.[1]

2.  References to another part of your paper.[2]

3.  Presentation of an opinion differing from one expressed in the
    text.[3]

4.  Explanation or definition of terms.[4]


[1]The next section in the text will show an additional way of commenting on
material without using a footnote like this.

[2]The location of footnotes is explained on page 114.

[3]Many modern researchers, particularly in the sciences and education, prefer a
slightly different form. (It will be illustrated later.)

[4]A footnote literally means at the "foot" or bottom of material being cited. All
kinds of documentary notations are called "notes."

## Writing the Notes

When you write the first draft of your paper, it is convenient to put the documentation information in parentheses immediately after the passage requiring it. Use whatever abbreviations you need for brevity, as long as you can understand the information later. One passage from the first draft of the sample research paper in this book looked like this:

```
The woman goes to look in the nets ''with the swift surge of

wonder that swept through her at any new sight.'' (''Please

Don't . . . ,'' p. 71) In this quest for new experiences,

she reflects the Roslyn of the earlier story.
```

As you can see on page 182, the full documentation shows the complete name of the short story from which the phrase was taken. There, the citation is number 4; it is the note for the passage on page 174.

There cannot be any one rule about the number of documentary notes that ought to be in a paper of any given length, for the worth of a work cannot be measured by the quantity of references. Some people feel that unless you have at least one footnote on each page of a research paper you may be writing more from supposition than from research. However, if you load a paper with footnotes, it may seem that you have done no thinking of your own but simply gathered the words of others without evaluation. When you revise the paper, it's a good idea to weigh every documentation and be sure you can justify its inclusion.

## Numbering System

Documented passages used as illustration throughout this book show the conventions of a numbering system. The numbers (for all but in-text documentation) appear at *the end of material being acknowledged,* whether that is the middle of the sentence or the end of one. Numbers are put *after* appropriate punctuation marks such as quotation marks or periods. The only mark that they precede is a dash. Type (or write) the number one-half space above the regular line.

Each number within the text of a written paper has a corresponding number *preceding the explanation* that is the documentation. That is, if you are using footnotes, each number will appear twice on a page: once in the text and a second time at the bottom of the page. If you use a page of notes at the end of a paper, the number will appear once on the page of text and again on the page headed "Notes" at the end of the text.

Do not put a period after the numbers in either the text or the corresponding documentation.

Number documenting notes consecutively throughout the paper, as previously stated. If you should write an especially long paper, with several chapters or divisions, you may use one set of numbers for each section, as this book does for each chapter. (Still another system—starting the first footnote of each page with the number 1—is acceptable but not widely used.)

## Form of Documentation Notes

Notes are typed double-spaced. Indent five spaces and use the same note number (still without a period and one-half space above the line of type) as in the text; then type the appropriate wording. (The *MLA Handbook* recommends leaving one space between the number and the first word.) Begin the note with a capital letter even if the first word is not a proper noun or if the citation will not be a grammatically complete sentence. The second and succeeding lines of the note begin at the left-hand margin of the text. End each note with a period. Double-space between successive notes on a page. Allow the usual bottom margin.

Since you have already recorded bibliographic information (on the preliminary bibliography cards), it may help you to remember that in a note, an author's name is given in usual order—that is, first name and then last name. There are some differences in punctuation between a note and a bibliographic entry. Actual page numbers used in getting information appear in notes (but not in a bibliography).

### First References

Notes give information about sources in a research paper. Therefore, the best form for them is one that conveys all the required information in the simplest, least distracting way. More information is needed the first time a source is identified than in subsequent references to it.

The first reference **for a book** gives the author and title of a work, the place of publication, the publisher and date of publication, as well as the specific page or pages on which the information used is located. Commas separate the three parts of a note: the author, all publication information, and the precise pages used.

> ³Arthur Miller, The Misfits (New York: Viking, 1961), pp. 91–92.

The standard first reference form **for articles** includes the name of the author (when available), the publication in which it appears, the date of publication, and the page on which the article is found. (Newspaper columns are indicated after the page.) Note that commas separate all these items.

> ⁶Henry Popkin, ''Arthur Miller Out West,'' Commentary, 31 May 1961, p. 435.

> ¹¹Bosley Crowther, ''The Misfits Reviewed,'' New York Times, 2 February 1961, p. 24, col. 2.

The symbol "p.," abbreviating page ("pp." for the plural), is omitted when a volume number for a magazine is given. If pages are numbered successively in a volume rather than by individual issue or publication date, the volume number should also be given before the publication date and the abbreviation for "page" should be omitted.

> ⁸Hollis Alpert, ''Arthur Miller: Screenwriter,'' Saturday Review, 44 (4 February 1961), 27.

## Subsequent References

Once the full information about a source has been presented, subsequent references should be given in shortened form. Make sure that they are clear, as well as brief. The simplest form is to record only the name of the author and a page number.

> ¹⁵Huftel, pp. 170–171.

If you are using more than one work by the same author, you must include the title of the work in the subsequent reference.

> ¹⁴Miller, Misfits, pp. 87–88.

If an author's name is mentioned in the text, you need not repeat it. For instance, in the sample research paper later in this book you will see a passage that says:

```
Gay . . . thinks of her ''eastern surprise at everything they
did and saw and said,''² thus giving us . . .
```

The footnote reads

```
²Page 90.
```

The text is the same as one already cited as a first reference, so this subsequent reference simply gives the page from which this quotation was taken. Note that in the previous example "Miller" could be omitted if the author's name appeared in the text.

Titles may also be shortened in subsequent references. For instance, *The Research Paper: Form and Content* may be shortened to *Research Paper*.

"Ibid.," a shortened form (as indicated by the period used with abbreviations) of the Latin *ibidem,* meaning "in the same place," was long used to show the source of one note was identical with the one directly preceding it, though the page number was not necessarily the same.

```
²Ibid., p. 90.
```

Although ordinarily all foreign words and phrases are underlined to indicate italics, the term is now so frequently used that the underlining is unnecessary. However, since it is the first word after the footnote number, it should begin with a capital letter.

A form now preferred to "Ibid." for a subsequent reference is simply to give the page number, as illustrated in the sample research paper on page 182.

```
²Page 90.
```

Instead of using either a footnote or endnote, with the requisite superscript numbers, the page number of a subsequent reference might be put in parentheses as in:

```
As Leonard observes (on page 62), ''It is too bad . . .''
```

# Special Problems in Documentation

### One Author Quoted by Another

As you prepared material, you may have found that sometimes **one author quoted another.** Here is one such problem that needs documentation.

John Stuart Katz collected some essays for a book titled *Perspectives on the Study of Film* published by Little, Brown and Company of Boston in 1971. One of the essays in it (pp. 200–214) is "The New Languages" by Edmund Carpenter. In that essay (p. 206), Carpenter quotes Bela Balazs from p. 48 of *his* work, *Theory of Film* published by Roy Publishers of New York in 1953 and Denis Dobson of London in 1952. (No page reference to the passage is given for the London edition.)

As the author of the statement, Balazs must be given credit. However, so must Carpenter for his essay and Katz for his book. Credit is given in that order and the citation should be handled in this way:

**The Quotation:**
Although we sit in our seats, we do not see Romeo and Juliet
from there. We look up into Juliet's balcony . . . the film
manifests its absolute artistic novelty.

**The Citation:**
   [12]Bela Balazs, Theory of Film(New York: Roy Publishers, 1953), p. 48. Quoted by Edmund Carpenter, ''The New Languages,'' in Perspectives on the Study of Film, ed. John Stuart Katz (Boston: Little, Brown, 1971), p. 206.

### Casebooks and Sourcebooks

**Casebooks or sourcebooks** are popular sources of information. They are useful because an editor has done an important scholarly job of bringing together a collection of reference material that the reader might otherwise have to seek out (and sometimes may not have access to). The material used from the casebook or sourcebook requires that both the original author of the work and the editor of the book you are using be given credit. Here is how to handle such a citation:

**The Quotation:**

According to Bernard M. Knieger, ''Class response to an analysis of 'Humpty Dumpty' is guaranteed: the very idea of analyzing so simple a poem is amusing.''[13]

**The Citation:**

[13]From ''Humpty Dumpty,'' in <u>Literary Symbolism,</u> ed. Maurice Beebe (Belmont, Calif.: Wadsworth, 1960), p. 57. Originally published as ''Humpty Dumpty and Symbolism,'' <u>College English,</u> 30 (February 1959), 244.

Note that the author of the article is not repeated in the citation because it is in the text. Because *College English* is a periodical which has volume numbers, the specific volume, 30, appears before the date and no abbreviation for "page" is used.

Another kind of special problem might be encountered in using a casebook in which author and source are given, but not some other details. For example:

**The Quotation:**

Still another critic feels that ''. . . there emerges from this picture . . . a curiously agitating tension and a haunting sense of the wild impulses that move men.''[14]

**The Citation:**

[14]Bosley Crowther in the <u>New York Times,</u> 27 December 1951, [n.p.], in <u>Focus on Rashomon,</u> ed. Donald S. Richie (Englewood Cliffs, N.J.: Prentice-Hall, 1972), p. 44.

Keep in mind that the point of these, and all other, citations is to give a reader enough information to be able to consult the same sources you used.

If you go from the casebook or sourcebook directly to the original location of the material and then use the original source, you will only need to cite the source actually used.

## Readers

**Readers** (collections of essays, articles, or stories) may provide you with research information, as one did for the student who wrote the sample research paper in Appendix C. As you can see there, Eric Mottram wrote a piece that was reprinted in the Robert Corrigan book. Only the Corrigan book appears in the bibliography (page 183), and the citation on page 182 gives credit to both Mottram, the original source, and Corrigan.

> [17]Eric Mottram, ''Arthur Miller: The Development of a Political Dramatist in America,'' in <u>Arthur Miller: A Collection of Essays,</u> ed. Robert W. Corrigan (Englewood Cliffs, N.J.: Prentice-Hall, 1969).

## Plays

**Plays** are customarily documented in a slightly different way from other printed matter, especially if the play is composed of scenes as well as acts.

> <u>Hamlet</u> IV.ii.62

means that the quotation or reference is to Shakespeare's *Hamlet,* Act 4, Scene 2, Line 62. Any edition of the play may be used to locate that source. Citations for plays that do not have numbered lines or acts should give the page location, as well as other publication information, including the edition used.

## Biblical Quotations

**Biblical quotations** or references are documented by book, chapter, and verse.

> Ruth 7.17

or

> Ruth vii.17

means that the Book of Ruth, chapter 7, verse 17 was cited. The King James version of the Bible is assumed, unless another edition is specified, as in

> Ruth 7.17 (Revised Standard Version)

Books in the Bible are not customarily underlined or put in quotation marks, either in the text, a note, or bibliography. These references are usually handled as in-text documentation in parentheses and, once the translation or edition is established, it need not be repeated in each citation within a paper.

## Nonprint Media

**Nonprint media** such as films, audiotapes, videotapes, and interviews must also be acknowledged if they are sources of either quotations or ideas in the research paper. Consult Appendix B (pages 154–157 and 165–167) for specific forms to use.

# Forms for Natural and Social Sciences

The natural and social sciences use a slightly different form for both first and subsequent references. If you write a paper for a course in those disciplines and are asked to follow the form usually observed in published papers, use only the author's last name and date of publication in parentheses within the text. (Often the author's name is part of the text, so the date of publication alone is in parentheses.)

```
''Deschooling,'' in which formal schooling is eliminated or
greatly curtailed (Illich, 1971), is only one of several
possibilities suggested for changing current educational
patterns.
```

                                        or

```
Illich (1971) suggests ''deschooling,'' in which formal
schooling is eliminated or greatly curtailed; it is only
one of several possibilities suggested for changing current
educational patterns.
```

At the end of the research paper text is a page headed "References" on which the book by Illich would be listed, in alphabetical order, as in any other bibliography.

> Illich, Ivan. <u>Deschooling Society.</u> New York: Harper and Row, 1970.

If an author has published two (or more) pieces in the same year, both of which are cited in the research paper text, you need to indicate which reference is which. One common way of doing so is to assign a letter to the date:

> (Knox, 1972a)
>
> (Knox, 1972b)

Then, the two items are designated in the same way within the bibliography or reference list:

> Knox, A. B. ''Continuing Professional Education: Need, Scope, and Setting.'' <u>The Illinois Education Review,</u> Summer 1972a, <u>1,</u> 8–18.
>
> Knox, A. B. ''Achieving the Fifth Freedom.'' <u>Adult Leadership,</u> September 1972b, <u>21,</u> 100–104.

The underlined numerals in the references show volume numbers of the publication, a form sometimes used.

# 9

# Final Presentation

The paper is written, the revisions made, and now you are ready to do the last few tasks that will present your paper in the best possible way to a teacher or other reader.

The completed research paper customarily consists of a title page, an outline of the paper, the text (with illustrative materials such as pictures, graphs, or charts), the notes, and a bibliography, sometimes annotated. (Some teachers may feel that a term paper does not need a title page and prefer that you put the title only on the first page of the paper—this method is preferred by the *MLA Handbook*.) In addition, there may be a preface. Business, technical, and scientific research works sometimes have a synopsis or abstract of the study. Appendices containing material relevant to the research and illustrating or supporting it are sometimes added.

A blank *end sheet* after the bibliography (or appendices, if you have any) gives your research paper a neat and finished appearance. Some instructors also appreciate having such a place on which to write comments about your paper.

Most instructors are glad to have you *securely fasten together* the pages of your completed research work. Generally, staple the pages in the upper left corner or along the left side to make a booklet. Or, fasten your papers inside one of the many inexpensive covers or binders available; they protect your work as well as hold it together, and many instructors prefer receiving research papers in such binders. However, some instructors prefer that you fasten the pages with a paper clip so a sheet of endnotes is easy to remove and put next to the research paper for quick reference during reading. Follow your instructor's preference for submission of fastened or paper-clipped pages.

# Typing

Type the research paper if at all possible. (Some instructors will require that it be typed; others will accept handwritten papers. Be sure to ask your instructor about requirements.) Use standard $8\frac{1}{2}$ x 11-inch white typing paper of a good quality for your research paper. "Erasable" paper is not recommended because it smudges easily. Never use onion skin or other thin paper that is difficult to handle or on which wording is hard to read.

Type the text double-spaced on only one side of each page and leave adequate margins all around; one inch on all sides is usual. Indent the beginning of each new paragraph five spaces from the left margin. Do not use extra-wide margins or skip extra spaces in order to make your paper appear longer than it actually is.

Number the pages consecutively throughout the text. It is not necessary to number the first page, but if you do so, place the number at the bottom of the text and centered on the page. Put succeeding page numbers of each sheet in the upper right-hand corner; your name and course number may be put below each page number. If you have material in addition to an outline appearing before the text, number those pages with small Roman numerals.

Footnotes, if used, should be typed single-spaced; endnotes should be typed double-spaced. Double-space between notes.

Long quotations should be typed double-spaced (or single-spaced if your teacher prefers). You should indent a long quotation ten spaces in from the left margin.

# Proofreading

After typing the text and other parts of your research paper, proofread each page carefully. An author is responsible for the accuracy of all work, including spelling and punctuation (which may contain typing errors). Correct any errors as neatly as possible. White-out or erase minor errors and make corrections in ink. Insert words between lines—very carefully—if they have been omitted in the typing. Any page that requires extensive corrections should be retyped.

## Title Page

The first page of your paper that a reader sees is the title page. It tells the subject of the paper, who wrote it, and information about why it was written—that is, usually the title of the course for which it was prepared, the name of the instructor, and sometimes the date on which it was due or was turned in. Consult your instructor for preference about the exact information required on the title page and the location of the information. (See an example in Appendix C.)

The title of the paper should be prominent on the page. It is usually centered on the page slightly above the middle of the sheet and is typed either in capital and small letters (recommended by the *MLA Handbook*) or in all capitals. Do not underline the title or put it in quotation marks. However, words that are ordinarily underlined (such as book titles or foreign words) or those customarily put in quotation marks (such as titles of stories and poems) should be underlined or enclosed in quotation marks as usual.

Your name, as author, should also be displayed prominently on the title page. Four spaces under the last line of the title and in the center of the page, write *by* and, two spaces below that, your name—also centered on the page.

Course information appears in the lower quarter of the page and may be typed either in the center or the lower right side. It should contain the designation of the course for which the paper was prepared and perhaps some other identifying information such as a sequence number. The name of the instructor for whom the paper was written is usually put on the second line, and, on the third line, the date on which the paper was handed in. Sometimes the name of the school also appears. Instructor preference will determine both content of the title page and location of its elements. (See an illustration of a title page in Appendix C.)

In an alternate form (recommended by the *MLA Handbook*), your name, your instructor's name, the course number, and the date are put in the upper right-hand corner in lieu of a title page, the title is centered and double-spaced; after quadruple spacing, the text begins.

## Outline

The outline from which the research paper was written is often included with the text so that an instructor may see at a glance the content and organization of your paper before reading it.

If your working outline is required as part of the presentation of the research paper, it should appear immediately after the title page (or the preface or summary, if either is used). Put the title of the paper at the top of the page and, four spaces below it, write the word THESIS in capital letters followed by a colon. Then write the thesis statement you used for your paper. Skip four spaces and begin the outline at the left margin of the page.

Double-space your outline if it is short, although you may single-space any sentence or statement that requires more than one line. Single spacing throughout a long outline is usually permissible because limiting the outline to a page (or two) makes it easier to read. Follow the outline form and spacing you have already read about in Chapter 6 (pages 85–87).

## The Text

When you type the text of your research paper, you will be following the conventions of style and documentation that you have read about in Chapter 8. (More detailed forms are in Appendix B, pages 158–168). Be sure that footnotes or endnotes are numbered consecutively and accurately throughout your paper and that each shows exactly where information was obtained: page, act, line, and so on.

Remember that underlining in typing or writing means that if the passage were set in type, those particular words would be italicized (as titles, foreign words or phrases, or words you want the reader to note particularly).

## Notes

Documentation is put on a page following the text of the research paper. (The page is usually not numbered.) Center the word "Notes" two inches from the top of the page, then skip three lines before beginning to type the first note. Remember to raise the number slightly before each entry and let that number correspond to the one in the text of the paper. (See the example on page 182). This format is the one preferred by the *MLA Handbook* for use in research papers.

## Illustrative Materials

If your research paper includes graphs, charts, pictures, or other kinds of illustration, you will, of course, acknowledge the source of any material that is not original. Captions or titles may appear above or below the material; there is no rule governing their location except that you be consistent in placing the information. Sources of charts, graphs, and other material not original may be acknowledged in the text, in the caption, or in a note.

Put illustrative materials as close as you can to the portion of the text they illustrate. Remember that everything in your research paper should be understood easily by anyone who reads the paper, and anything you can do to make that reading easier is desirable.

## Bibliography

The bibliography is a list acknowledging *all* the sources you have used in preparing your research paper. Even if you obtain information from only one page of a book, that book should be in the bibliography. However, if you consulted a source but did *not* use any information from it, do not record it in the bibliography (unless specifically requested by your instructor to do so). Be sure that every item cited in the text appears in the bibliography—though every item in the bibliography will not necessarily be cited in a note. Do not number the bibliography page.

A bibliography is easy to prepare if you have put complete information on your preliminary bibliography cards and kept all the source cards you made while seeking information. Arrange the cards in alphabetical order by the author's (or editor's) last name; if an author is represented by more than one item, arrange the works in alphabetical order by title. Then, instead of repeating the name when you type the bibliography, substitute a long dash and begin the second title under the first, like this:

```
Montague, Ashley. The Nature of Human Aggression. New York:
    Oxford, 1976.

———. Race and I.Q. New York: Oxford, 1975.
```

Notice that the bibliographic form uses **hanging indentation**; that is, the first line of each entry begins at the left margin and subsequent lines are indented five spaces. Entries are double-spaced (preferred by the MLA) as in the sample student paper in Appendix C. Or, they may be single-spaced with double space between entries. Note that entries in a bibliography are never numbered. No distinction is made between a hardbound and a paperbound book although the publisher of the edition you used will often be an indication.

Most bibliographies are arranged in a single alphabetical listing of all sources. Especially long lists, however, such as those taking up two or more pages, may be divided in either of two ways: (1) by separating primary sources from secondary sources, or (2) by separating books from periodicals.

**Unsigned materials** are listed by title, and all alphabetizing is by first word in the title. If the first word is an article (*a, an,* or *the*), alphabetize by the second word.

    ''Senate Votes Unanimously to Revise Copyright Law.'' School
        Library Journal, April 1976, p. 11.

    ''A World Poll on the 'Quality of Life.' '' New York Times,
        7 November 1976, p. 2, cols. 3-4.

Page numbers on which magazine and newspaper articles appear (as well as section and/or column designations for ease of location) are customarily recorded in the bibliography, even though your information may not have come from each page. (Page numbers actually used for reference appear in the footnotes, never in the bibliography.)

**Book**

    Jaffe, Rona. Family Secrets. New York: Simon and Schuster,
        1974.

**Scientific Article**

    Vinson, J. S. ''Inexpensive Laser Communication Apparatus.''
        American Journal of Physics, 44:111 (January 1976).

**Article**

    Burns, John F. ''Black Nations Call War Only Way to Gain
        Majority Rule in Rhodesia.'' New York Times, 7 November
        1976, p. 1, cols. 1-2 and p. 21, col.1.

See Appendix B for details of all bibliographic forms.

## Annotation

An annotation tells what is important or characteristic about a source. If your instructor requires an annotated bibliography, the annotation begins right after the period ending the bibliographic entry.

Annotations are particularly helpful to anyone who wishes to consult the sources you have used in preparing your research paper. Since they tell the contents of each source, a reader can decide which ones are of special interest. An annotation may do one or more of the following:

1.  *State the general content of the source:*

```
Supports the author's contention that Painted Veils was
written in six weeks.
```

2.  *Make a judgment about the source:*

```
A lucid explanation of the Theory of Forms.
```

3.  *Point out valuable properties* or qualities of the source in addition to the text:

```
Contains photographs by the author.
```

4.  *Note the viewpoint or bias of the author of the source:*

```
Prefers Arnold's viewpoint rather than Huxley's.
```

5.  *Tell something about the author* of the source, such as stature in the field:

```
By a pupil and leading U.S. exponent of Freud.
```

Look at the annotated bibliographies in some of the sources you use for your research work, and you may discover even other kinds of information an annotation may contain.

As these examples show, statements in the form of sentence fragments (the title or author is an implied subject) rather than complete sentences are the custom in annotations; unless you are specifically instructed otherwise, you may use either sentences or fragments—as long as you are consistent throughout the bibliography. Begin each annotation with a capital letter and end it with a period, even if you choose to write fragments instead of sentences. Also, keep each annotation brief; one or two remarks will suffice.

Begin typing an annotation two spaces after the conclusion of its bibliographic entry and on the same line; maintain the indentation used for the entry.

**Example:**

Miller, Arthur. I Don't Need You Any More. New York: Viking, 1967. A collection of short stories which includes ''Please Don't Kill Anything'' and ''The Misfits.''

## Preface

Most undergraduate papers do not require a preface or statement of purpose. However, ask your instructor if one should be included as part of the presentation of your research work. If it is, you should know that a preface is a brief introduction, usually half a page long, headed by the word "Preface" or "Purpose" typed in capital and lowercase letters as if it were a title at the top of the page (be consistent; if you type the title of the paper all in capital letters, you should do the same for this kind of heading). The preface tells what is contained in the paper itself. Some prefaces also state the purpose of the research.

## Synopsis or Abstract

This, too, is usually not included in undergraduate papers though it might be expected with some research done in the natural or social sciences. Ask your instructor about including it in the presentation if you are in doubt. The synopsis or abstract is a summary of the *contents* of your investigation. It tells (usually in a page or less) what is found in more detail within the text of the research paper and is therefore different from a preface, which is usually more general and stresses the purpose for which an investigation was undertaken rather than the results discovered. If your presentation requires it, head a page "Abstract" or "Synopsis" in capital and lowercase letters, centered, and write the summary of the contents of the paper in sentences and paragraphs.

## Appendix

Few student papers need to include the additional material illustrating or amplifying a text that constitutes an appendix (or appendices). An appendix enables the author to include such material without interrupting the text itself. For example, a series of charts or tables illustrating demographic changes might better be shown in an appendix than in the text of the paper, even though such charts were discussed in the text.

In this book there are several appendices to accommodate useful information you will need as reference for your own work on the research paper: some reference works available in libraries, examples of various kinds of bibliographic and footnote forms, and a student research paper to use as an example for your own work.

# A

# A Selected List of Reference Works Available in Libraries

It is impossible to list all the reference materials available in even a moderate-sized library. Reference books are updated or added. Periodicals begin or cease publication. New information and retrieval systems are being installed as computers are used more extensively. So, as soon as any list is compiled for a book like this, it is out of date. (Moreover, any such list would be far longer than this entire book.) What follows, then, is a *selected* listing of sources found in most libraries, which students are likely to find helpful in preparing research papers.

Most of the materials listed here are either published as books or are indexes of published periodical articles. But it is possible to find unpublished materials, too—for example, by consulting the ERIC (Educational Resources Information Center) indexes published by government-funded centers that gather, catalog, and reproduce materials for educators.

Every business, profession, and hobby has at least one—and usually many more—journals, magazines, or newspapers published for people concerned with it. They range from the *American Waterworks Association Journal* to *Volume Feeding Management*—with others before, after, and in between. Obviously, it would be impossible to list all these journals, and it is not necessary to do so. Your own library will have a listing of those to which it subscribes.

The following selected list is offered as a guide to the many materials available. It is by no means complete or exhaustive in any category, and the best procedure is to use the list as a guide when consulting each library for additional sources of information. The listing here is divided into four main groups with numerous subgroups:

1. General Reference Works
   a. General
   b. Atlases
   c. Biography
   d. Dictionaries
   e. Encyclopedias
   f. Periodical Indexes

2. Natural Sciences
   a. General
   b. Agriculture
   c. Applied Science
   d. Biology
   e. Chemistry
   f. Geology
   g. Physics and Mathematics

3. Social Sciences
   a. General
   b. Business
   c. Economics

   d. Education
   e. Geography
   f. History
   g. Political Science
   h. Psychology
   i. Sociology

4. Humanities
   a. Art and Architecture
   b. Literature
   c. Music and Dance
   d. Philosophy and Religion

1. General Reference Works

   a. General
      *Britannica Book of the Year.*   Since 1938
      *Dissertation Abstracts International.*   Since 1967
           [Formerly *Dissertation Abstracts.*   Since 1938]
      *Europa Yearbook: A World Survey.* 2 vols.   1975
      *Facts on File: World News Digest.*   Since 1940
      *Familiar Quotations.*   1968
      *Home Book of Proverbs, Maxims and Familiar Phrases.*   1948
      *Information Please Almanac.*   Since 1947
      *The Reader's Adviser.*   1969
      *The Reader's Encyclopedia.*   1965
      *Statesman's Year Book.*   Since 1864
      *Statistical Abstract of the United States.*   Since 1878
      *United Nations Yearbook.*   Since 1948
      *World Almanac and Book of Facts.*   Since 1868

   b. Atlases
      *Atlas of American History.*   1943
      *Atlas of Early American History.*   1976
      *Columbia-Lippincott Gazetteer of the World.*   1952
      *Commercial Atlas and Marketing Guide.*   1965
      *Encyclopaedia Britannica World Atlas.*   1961
      *McGraw-Hill International Atlas.*   1968
      *National Geographic Atlas of the World.*   1970
      *The Times Atlas of the World.*   5 vols., 1955–59
      *Universal World Atlas.*   1960

   c. Biography
      *American Men and Women of Science.*   6 vols., 1971
      · *Biography Index: A Cumulative Index to Biographical Material in Books and Magazines.*   Since 1946

*Chambers' Biographical Dictionary.*   1968
*Chambers' Dictionary of Scientists.*   1952
*Current Biography: Who's News and Why.*   Since 1940
*Dictionary of American Biography.*   21 vols., 1958
*Dictionary of National Biography.*   24 vols., 1885–1950
*Directory of American Scholars.*   Since 1942
*International Who's Who.*   Since 1936
*The National Cyclopedia of American Biography.*   69 vols., since 1891
*New Century Cyclopedia of Names.*   3 vols., 1954
*The New York Times Biographical Edition.*   Since 1969
*Twentieth Century Authors.*   With supplements, 1942
*Webster's Biographical Dictionary.*   1943
*Who's Who.*   Since 1848
*Who's Who in America.*   Since 1899

d. Dictionaries
*Chemical Dictionary.*   1969
*A Comprehensive Dictionary of Psychological and Psychoanalytical Terms.*   1958
*The Concise Oxford Dictionary of Current English.*   1964
*Dictionary of American English on Historical Principles.*   4 vols., 1936–1944
*Dictionary of Business Terms.*   1952
*Dictionary of Education.*   1959
*Dictionary of Scientific Terms* (biological sciences).   1960
*Dorland's Illustrated Medical Dictionary.*   1965
*The International Dictionary of Applied Mathematics.*   1960
*Black's Law Dictionary.*   1951
*New Standard Dictionary of the English Language.*   1963
*Oxford English Dictionary.*   13 vols. and supp., 1933
*Roget's International Thesaurus.*   1969
*Stedman's Medical Dictionary.*   1972
*Webster's New Dictionary of Synonyms.*   1968
*Webster's Third New International Dictionary.*   1961

e. Encyclopedias
*Encyclopaedia Britannica.* (*Britannica* 3), 15th ed., 30 vols., 1974
*Encyclopedia Americana.*   30 vols., 1975
*Collier's Encyclopedia.*   24 vols., 1970
*Columbia Encyclopedia.*   1 vol., 1963
*New International Encyclopedia.*   23 vols., 1922

f. Periodical Indexes

*Applied Science and Technology Index.*   Since 1958

*Art Index.*   Since 1929

*Bibliographic Index: A Cumulative Bibliography of Bibliographies.*   Since 1938

*Book Review Digest.*   Since 1905

*Business Periodicals Index.*   Since 1958

*Education Index.*   Since 1929

*Essay and General Literature Index.*   Since 1900

*Humanities Index.*   Since 1974

*Index to American Doctoral Dissertations.*   Since 1957

*Index to Book Reviews in the Humanities.*   Since 1960

*Industrial Arts Index.*   1913–1957 (Superseded by *Applied Science and Technology Index.*   Since 1958)

*International Index to Periodicals.*   1907–1964 (Superseded by *Social Sciences and Humanities Index.*   Since 1965)

*International Nursing Index.*   Since 1966

*The Music Index.*   Since 1949

*MLA International Bibliography.*   Since 1963

*New York Times Index.*   Since 1851

*Nineteenth Century Readers' Guide, 1890–1899.*   1945

*Poole's Index to Periodical Literature, 1802–1906.*   7 vols.

*Public Affairs Information Service.*   Since 1915

*Readers' Guide to Periodical Literature.*   Since 1900

*Social Sciences Index.*   Since 1974

*Social Sciences and Humanities Index.*   1965–1974. (Superseded by *Social Sciences Index* and *Humanities Index*)

*Technical Book Review Index.*   Since 1917

*United States Catalog: Books in Print.*   Since 1928

*United States Government Publications.*   Since 1895

*Vertical File Index.*   Since 1935

2. Natural Sciences

a. General

*A Guide to the History of Science.*   1952

*Guide to the Selection of Computer-Based Science and Technology Reference Services in the U.S.A.*   1969

*McGraw-Hill Encyclopedia of Science and Technology.*   15 vols., 1966

*Science Reference Sources.*   1969

*Van Nostrand's Scientific Encyclopedia.*   1958

b. Agriculture

*Bibliography of Agriculture.*   Since 1942

*Biological and Agricultural Index.*   Since 1916
*Index to Publications of the U.S. Department of Agriculture.*
    1901–1925, 1932
*Yearbook of Agriculture.*   Since 1894

c.  Applied Science
    *Applied Science and Technology Index.*   Since 1958
    *Engineering Encyclopedia.*   2 vols., 1963
    *Engineering Index.*   Since 1884
    *History of Magic and Experimental Science.*   8 vols., 1923–
        1958
    *Industrial Engineering Handbook.*   1963
    *Technical Publications.*   1955
    *U.S. Government Research Reports.*   Since 1946

d.  Biology
    *Biological Abstracts.*   Since 1926
    *Biological and Agricultural Index.*   Since 1916
    *Dictionary of Scientific Terms . . . in Biology, Botany, Zo-
        ology, Anatomy, Cytology, Embryology, Physiology.*   1960
    *Encyclopedia of the Biological Sciences.*   1961
    *Gray's Anatomy.*   1973
    *Guide to the Literature of the Zoological Sciences.*   1967
    *Index Medicus.*   Since 1927
    *The Merck Manual.*   Since 1899
    *Physician's Desk Reference.*   Since 1947
    *Progress in Biophysics and Biophysical Chemistry.*   Since 1950
        (Now *Progress in Biophysics and Molecular Biology.*)
    *Scientific, Medical, and Technical Books.*   1958
    *Seventy-Five Years of Medical Progress, 1878–1953.*   1954

e.  Chemistry
    *Chemical Abstracts.*   Since 1907
    *Chemical Publications: Their Nature and Use.*   1965
    *Dictionary of Applied Chemistry.*   12 vols., 1937–56
    *Encyclopedia of Chemical Technology.*   18 vols., 1963
    *Handbook of Chemistry and Physics.*   1975–1976
    *Lange's Handbook of Chemistry.*   1973
    *Van Nostrand's Chemical Annual.*   Since 1907

f.  Geology
    *Annotated Bibliography of Economic Geology.*   Since 1928
    *Basic Geology for Science and Engineering.*   1959
    *Bibliography of North American Geology.*   Since 1906

*Geological Abstracts.*   Since 1953
*Minerals Yearbook.*   Since 1933

g. Physics and Mathematics
*Annual Review of Nuclear Science.*   Since 1952
*Barlow's Tables.*   1958
*Dictionary of Named Effects and Laws in Chemistry, Physics and Mathematics.*   1961
*Encyclopaedic Dictionary of Physics.*   9 vols., 1961
*Guide to the Literature of Mathematics and Physics.*   1958
*Handbook of Chemistry and Physics.*   Since 1914
*An International Bibliography of Atomic Energy.*   Since 1949
*Mathematics Dictionary.*   1968
*Reviews of Modern Physics.*   Since 1929

3. Social Sciences

a. General
*Checklist of Books and Pamphlets in the Social Sciences.*   1956
*Dictionary of Social Science.*   1959
*Encyclopaedia of the Social Sciences.*   8 vols., 1930
*A Guide to the Study of the United States of America.*   1960
*An International Encyclopedia of the Social Sciences.*   17 vols., 1968
*A Reader's Guide to the Social Sciences.*   Since 1959
*Sources of Information in the Social Sciences.*   1964
*Worldmark Encyclopedia of the Nations.*   5 vols., 1967

b. Business
*Business Information: How to Find and Use It.*   1955
*Business Periodicals Index.*   Since 1958
*Commodity Year Book.*   Since 1939
*Dun and Bradstreet Corporate Management.*   Since 1967
*Dun's Review.*   Since 1893.
*Foreign Commerce Yearbook.*   Since 1933
*Moody's Manual of Investments.*   Since 1929
*Poor's Register of Corporations, Directors and Executives, United States and Canada.*   Since 1928
*Sources of Business Information.*   1964
*Standard and Poor's Corporation Records.*   Since 1928
*Survey of Current Business.*   Since 1921
*Thomas' Register of American Manufacturers.*   Since 1905
*Wall Street Journal Index.*   Since 1958

c. Economics
   *Dictionary of Modern Economics.* 1965
   *Economic Almanac.* Since 1940
   *Review of Economics and Statistics.* Since 1919

d. Education
   *Biennial Survey of Education.* Since 1916–18
   *Current Index to Journals in Education.* Since 1969
   *A Cyclopedia of Education.* 5 vols., 1911–13
   *Dictionary of Education.* 1959
   *Education Directory.* 1912
   *Encyclopedia of Educational Research.* 1960
   *ERIC Research in Education.* Since 1966
   *How to Locate Educational Information and Data.* 1958
   *Who's Who in American Education.* Since 1928.

e. Geography
   *Chisholm's Handbook of Commercial Geography.* 1960
   *The Climates of the Continents.* 1961
   *Geographical Bibliography for all the Major Nations of the
       World.* 1959
   *National Geographical Index.* Since 1899
   *Webster's Geographical Dictionary.* 1959

f. History
   *American Historical Review.* Since 1895
   *Bibliographies in American History.* 1942
   *Cambridge Ancient History.* 12 vols., 1923–39
   *Cambridge Medieval History.* 8 vols., 1911–36
   *Dictionary of American History.* 6 vols., 1942–61
   *Encyclopedia of American History.* 1961
   *Encyclopedia of World History.* 1952
   *Guide to Historical Literature.* 1961
   *Harvard Guide to American History.* 1954
   *Historical Abstracts.* Since 1955
   *History of American Life: A Social, Cultural, and Economic
       Analysis.* 13 vols., 1929–44
   *New Cambridge Modern History.* 12 vols., 1957
   *The New Learned History for Ready Reference, Reading, and
       Research.* 12 vols., 1922–24
   *Writings on American History.* 1961

g. Political Science
   *American Political Science Review.* Since 1906
   *American Political Terms.* 1962

*Congressional Record.*   Since 1873
*Dictionary of American Politics.*   1968
*Documents on American Foreign Relations.*   Since 1939
*Elements of Government.*   1960
*Encyclopedia of Modern World Politics.*   1950
*Index to Legal Periodicals.*   Since 1909
*Municipal Year Book.*   Since 1934
*Political Handbook of the World.*   Since 1927
*Public Affairs Information Service.*   Since 1915
*Statesman's Yearbook.*   Since 1864

h. Psychology
*American Journal of Psychology.*   Since 1887
*A Comprehensive Dictionary of Psychological and Psycho-
    analytical Terms.*   1958
*Encyclopedia of Psychology.*   1956
*Handbook of Social Psychology.*   5 vols., 1968
*List of Books in Psychology.*   1958
*Phrenology: Fad and Science: A 19th-Century American Cru-
    sade.*   1955
*Professional Problems in Psychology.*   1953
*Psychological Abstracts.*   Since 1927
*Psychological Bulletin.*   Since 1904

i. Sociology
*American Journal of Sociology.*   Since 1895
*American Sociological Review.*   Since 1936
*Bibliography of Researchers in Rural Sociology.*   1957
*General Index: Annual Reports—U.S. Bureau of American
    Ethnology, 1876–1931.*   48 vols.
*Handbook of Sociology.*   1941
*Social Forces.*   Since 1922
*Social Science Abstracts.*   5 vols., 1929–33
*Social Work Year Book.*   Since 1929
*Sociological Abstracts.*   Since 1953
*Sociology and Social Work in the United States: A Bibliogra-
    phy.*   1959

4. Humanities

a. Art and Architecture
*American Art Annual.*   Since 1898
*Art in the Western World.*   1963
*Art Index.*   Since 1929
*Art through the Ages.*   1959

*Costumes of the Western World.*   3 vols., 1951
*Encyclopedia of World Art.*   15 vols., 1959
*A History of Architecture on the Comparative Method.*   1961
*Who's Who in American Art.*   Since 1937

b.  Literature

*Abstracts of English Studies.*   Since 1958
*America in Fiction.*   1967
*American Authors, 1600–1900.*   1938
*American Literature.*   Since 1929
*Bibliography of American Literature.*   1959
*A Bibliography of North American Folklore and Folksong.*
     1961
*British Authors before 1800.*   1952
*British Authors of the 19th Century.*   1936
*Cambridge Bibliography of English Literature.*   4 vols., 1957
*Cambridge History of American Literature.*   4 vols., 1917–21
*Cambridge History of English Literature.*   15 vols., 1907–33
*Columbia Dictionary of Modern European Literature.*   1947
*The Concise Cambridge Bibliography of English Literature,*
     *600–1950.*   1965
*Dictionary of World Literature.*   1953
*Digests of Great American Plays.*   1961
*Directory of Newspapers and Periodicals.*   Since 1880
*Fiction Catalog.*   Since 1908
*Granger's Index to Poetry.*   1962
*Guide to English and American Literature.*   3rd ed., 1976
*History of American Magazines.*   5 vols., 1930–57
*A History of the English Novel.*   10 vols., 1924–39
*A History of English Poetry.*   6 vols., 1895–1910
*Index to Plays, 1800–1926.*   1935
*Journalist's Bookshelf.*   1961
*A Literary History of England.*   1967
*Literary History of the United States.*   3 vols., 1959
*Masterpieces of World Literature in Digest Form.*   1968
*Masterplots.*   11 vols., 1976
*New Century Classical Handbook.*   1962
*Oxford Companion to American Literature.*   1956
*Oxford Companion to Classical Literature.*   1948
*Oxford Companion to English Literature.*   1967
*Oxford Companion to French Literature.*   1959
*Play Index.*   4 vols., 1949–67
*PMLA* [*Publications of the Modern Language Association*].
     Since 1884

*Poetry Explication: A Checklist of Interpretations since 1925 of British and American Poems Past and Present.*   1962
*Princeton Encyclopedia of Poetry and Poetics.*   1975
*The Reader's Encyclopedia.*   1965
*Reference Books in the Mass Media.*   1962
*Short Story Index.*   4 vols., 1950–68
*Theatre and Allied Arts.*   1952
*Twentieth Century Short Story Explication.*   1967 and updates

c. Music and Dance
*Dance Encyclopedia.*   1967
*Dance Handbook.*   1959
*Encyclopedia of Jazz.*   1960
*Folksingers and Folksongs in America.*   1965
*Grove's Dictionary of Music and Musicians.*   9 vols., 1954
*Harvard Dictionary of Music.*   1969
*The International Cyclopedia of Music and Musicians.*   1964
*New Oxford History of Music.*   4 vols., 1960
*Oxford Companion to Music.*   1955
*Schirmer's Guide to Books on Music.*   1951

d. Philosophy and Religion
*Baker's Dictionary of Theology.*   1960
*Bible Atlases and Concordances.*   (A variety of titles available.)
*Concise Encyclopedia of Western Philosophy and Philosophers.*   1960
*Dictionary of the Bible.*   1963
*Dictionary of Philosophy and Psychology.*   3 vols., 1949
*Encyclopaedia of Religion and Ethics.*   7 vols., 1951
*Encyclopedia of Islam.*   4 vols., 1911–38
*Encyclopedia of Philosophy.*   8 vols., 1967
*The Golden Bough: A Study in Magic and Religion.*   12 vols., 1907–15
*Harper's Bible Dictionary.*   1959
*A History of American Philosophy.*   1963
*Index of Folk Literature.*   6 vols., 1955–58
*Index to Religious Periodical Literature.*   Since 1949
*International Bibliography of the History of Religions.*   Since 1954
*Jewish Encyclopedia.*   10 vols., 1939–44
*Journal of Philosophy.*   Since 1904
*Larousse Encyclopedia of Mythology.*   1959.
*New Catholic Encyclopedia.*   15 vols., 1967

*New Schaff-Herzog Encyclopedia of Religious Knowledge.*  12
    vols., 1908–12
*The Oxford Dictionary of the Christian Church.*   1958
*Philosophic Abstracts.*   Since 1939
*Philosophical Periodicals: An Annotated World List.*   1952
*Philosophical Review.*   Since 1892
*The Standard Jewish Encyclopedia.*   1962
*Religions, Mythologies, Folklores: An Annotated Bibliography.*
    1962
*Yearbook of American Churches.*   Since 1916

# B
# Bibliography and Documentation Forms

Bibliographies and documentation of the text have a very specific purpose in research papers: they tell a reader where you found your information. Thus, they establish the veracity of what you say and enable your reader to consult the sources you did should there be a desire to study your subject more thoroughly.

Tradition has established that a certain order and form govern bibliography and documentation in a research paper so that this important information can be conveyed easily and clearly. Readers accustomed to material with such citations expect the form to be followed, so it is a good idea to become accustomed to the standard usages. The forms shown on the following pages (and elsewhere in this book) are the ones recommended in the *MLA* [Modern Language Association] *Handbook for Writers of Research Papers, Theses, and Dissertations* (1977), a style accepted by most academic disciplines. (Variations used in many of the natural and social sciences are described on pages 124–125.)

## Conventions

The following conventions are observed in *both* bibliographies and other documentation:

1.  No distinction is made between a hardbound and a paperbound book.

2.  Long poems appearing in book form, such as *Paradise Lost,* are treated as books.

3. A dictionary is treated as a book, but the editor's name is omitted.

4. Months in periodical entries are written out in full, not abbreviated.

5. The Bible is not underlined (or italicized), nor are the names of books within it. The King James Version is assumed unless otherwise stated. (See also page 123.)

6. A subtitle is recorded as part of a title if it is short or if it is printed as part of the title on the cover or title page of a book. The subtitle is underlined (or italicized) because it is part of the title. (Example: *The Research Paper: Form and Content.*) The subtitle may be omitted from a footnote or endnote.

7. The names of publishers may be recorded in abbreviated form —that is, the names by which they are commonly called. Example: Wadsworth Publishing Co. Inc. may be recorded simply as "Wadsworth" unless an instructor specifies such usage is unacceptable.

## Bibliography

A bibliography records *all the sources* you consulted in preparing a research paper. Even if you used just one or two pages from a book, the entire volume should be shown in the bibliography. (See pp. 130–131 for the order of items in a bibliography and pp. 121–124 for special problems you may encounter.)

The information required in a bibliographic entry for *books* (see also Standard Forms, beginning on p. 148) includes the author's name, the title of the work, the name and city location of the publisher (the state, also, if the city isn't well known, and the publication date. Special information such as revisions, editions, volumes, multiple authors, editors, or illustrators is also recorded. All this information is available either on the catalog card or on the title page of the book. If you have been accurate in preparing the preliminary bibliography, you can now use the cards for the works actually consulted in order to write the bibliography. Do not show in the bibliography the page numbers you actually consulted within books.

If no publication date is shown, use the latest copyright date; if there are several copyright dates, use the last one. If the book lacks the information you need, use appropriate abbreviations enclosed in square brackets to show that you are aware of the omission: [n.p.] for "no place of publication evident" or "no name of publisher evident"; [n.d.] for "no date of publication available."

The information required in a bibliographic entry for *periodicals* (see Standard Forms beginning on page 153) is similar to that for books: author's name, title of the work, and date of publication. Also required are the title of the publication in which the article appears, the volume number (if pages are numbered consecutively throughout a year), and the pages on which the article may be found. All this is available either in a periodical index or on the masthead of a magazine (usually the same page on which the table of contents appears). The information on newspapers is best found in the issue itself if not in an appropriate index.

The information required in a bibliographic entry for *nonprint media* (see Forms beginning on page 155) emphasizes the speaker (in a radio or TV program or interview) only if that is the most important person; otherwise, the title of a film, filmstrip, or, sometimes, of a TV or radio program may take precedence. A composer's or performer's name takes precedence on most audiodiscs and audiotapes. Other information for nonprinted media used in the bibliography usually includes: source, date, time, other people involved in the work such as a narrator, director, or photographer.

*Hanging indentation form* is used for all bibliographic entries; that is, the first line of each entry begins at the left-hand margin and each succeeding line is indented five spaces from the left. Double-space between the lines, as shown in the sample research paper on page 183. (Single spacing has been used in the following section to allow the inclusion of a large number of examples.)

## Standard Forms for Bibliography

### Books

Book by Single Author

Sheehy, Gail. <u>Passages: Predictable Crises of Adult Life.</u>
     New York: Dutton, 1976.

Book by Two Authors

Gager, Nancy, and Cathleen Schurr. <u>Sexual Assault: Confronting Rape in America.</u> New York: Grosset and Dunlap, 1976.

## Book by Three or More Authors

Robbins, Martin D., William S. Dorn, and John E. Skelton.
Who Runs the Computer? Boulder, Col.: Westview Press,
1975.

## Organization or Institution as Author

Women in Transition, Inc. A Feminist Handbook on Separation
and Divorce. New York: Scribner's, 1975.

## Book in Collaboration

Fuller, R. B., in collaboration with E. J. Applewhite.
Synergetics: Explorations in the Geometry of Thinking.
New York: Macmillan, 1975.

## Book in which Illustrator Is Important

Lupo, Dom, illustrator. A Natural Way to Golf Power. Text
by Judy Rankin. New York: Harper and Row, 1976.

or

Rankin, Judy. A Natural Way to Golf Power. Illus. Dom Lupo.
New York: Harper and Row, 1976.

## Book, No Author Given

The Complete Dog Book. New York: Howell Book House, 1975.

## Author's Name Absent from Book But Known from Some Other Source

[Dynner, Eugene.] Camera Techniques. Miami: Travelogue Press,
1977.

## Book, Pseudonymous Author: Real Name Supplied

Twain, Mark [Samuel Langhorn Clemens]. The Adventures of
Huckleberry Finn. Boston: Riverside, 1968.

Book Condensation of Longer Work

Thompson, Thomas. <u>Lost.</u> Condensed from <u>Lost.</u> Pleasantville,
    N.Y.: The Reader's Digest Association, 1975.


Book, Single Editor or Compiler of a Collection

Meriam, Eve, comp. <u>Growing Up Female in America:</u> <u>Ten Lives.</u>
    New York: Doubleday, 1971.


Book, Multiple Editors or Compilers

Mednick, Martha T. S., et al., eds. <u>Women and Achievement:</u>
    <u>Social and Motivational Analyses.</u> New York: Halsted
    Press, 1975.


                              or


Mednick, Martha T. S., and others, eds. <u>Women and Achieve-</u>
    <u>ment: Social and Motivational Analyses.</u> New York:
    Halsted Press, 1975.


Anthology with No Editor Given

<u>A Malamud Reader.</u> Introd. Philip Rahv. New York: Farrar,
    Straus, and  Giroux, 1967.


Poem in Anthology

Ferland, Barbara. ''At the University.'' In <u>Caribbean Voices.</u>
    Selected by John Figueroa. New York: Robert B. Luce Co.,
    1973.


                              or


Brooks, Gwendolyn. ''Old Laughter,'' <u>Take Hold.</u> Nashville:
    Thomas Nelson, 1974.


Chapter in a Book by Author of Whole

Sartre, Jean-Paul. ''People's Theater and Bourgeois
    Theater.'' In <u>Sartre on Theater.</u> New York: Pantheon,
    1976.

Article, Chapter, Story, or Essay in a Collection (Not by Author)

King, Pat. ''A Strategy for Change.'' In <u>Affirmative</u> <u>Action</u>
     <u>for</u> <u>Women.</u> Ed. D. Jongeward and D. Scott. Reading, Mass.:
     Addison-Wesley, 1974.

Book Edited by Other Than Author of Contents

Cohen, Selma Jeanne. <u>A</u> <u>Sampler</u> <u>of</u> <u>Women's</u> <u>Studies:</u> <u>Papers.</u>
     Ed. Dorothy Gies McGuigan. Ann Arbor: University of
     Michigan, 1973.

Work of Author Contained in Collected Works

Webster, John. <u>The</u> <u>Tragedy</u> <u>of</u> <u>the</u> <u>Duchess</u> <u>of</u> <u>Malfi.</u> Vol. II
     of <u>The</u> <u>Complete</u> <u>Works</u> <u>of</u> <u>John</u> <u>Webster.</u> Ed. F. T. Lucas.
     London: Chatto and Windus, 1927.

Several-Volume Work under General Title, with Each Volume
Having Separate Title

Guthrie, W. K. C. <u>Plato:</u> <u>The</u> <u>Man</u> <u>and</u> <u>His</u> <u>Dialogues:</u> <u>Earlier</u>
     <u>Period.</u> Vol. IV of <u>A</u> <u>History</u> <u>of</u> <u>Greek</u> <u>Philosophy.</u>
     London: Cambridge University Press. 1975.

Book in Series Edited by Other Than Author

Kranz, Jurgen, ed. <u>Epidemics</u> <u>of</u> <u>Plant</u> <u>Diseases.</u> Ecological
     Studies. Eds. J. Jacobs et al. New York: Springer-
     Verlag, 1974.

Introduction by Other Than Author

Hamilton, James. <u>The</u> <u>Power</u> <u>to</u> <u>Probe:</u> <u>A</u> <u>Study</u> <u>of</u> <u>Congressional</u>
     <u>Investigations</u>. Introd. Sam J. Ervin, Jr. New York:
     Random House, 1976.

Work in Several Volumes

Magill, Frank N., ed. <u>Masterplots</u>. Vol. 6. Englewood Cliffs,
     N.J.: Prentice-Hall, 1976.

Translated Book, Known Author

Rank, Otto. <u>The Don Juan Legend.</u> Trans. David G. Winter.
    Princeton, N.J.: Princeton University Press, 1975.


Translated Book without Author Separate from Title

Hans <u>Bellmer/Sarane Alexandrian.</u> Trans. Jack Altman. New
    York: Rizzoli, 1972.


Edition of a Book

Hoar, William S. <u>General and Comparative Physiology.</u> 2nd ed.
    Englewood Cliffs, N.J.: Prentice-Hall, 1975.


Edition of a Book (Revised and Enlarged)

Dal Fabbro, Mario. <u>How to Build Modern Furniture.</u> Rev. and
    enl. ed. New York: McGraw Hill, 1976.


Signed Encyclopedia Article

Spencer, Sidney. ''Christian Mysticism.'' <u>Encyclopaedia
    Britannica.</u> 15th ed. (1974).


Unsigned Encyclopedia Article

''Maple Sugar Industry.'' <u>Encyclopedia Americana,</u> 1975.

[Volume and page numbers may be omitted from alphabetically arranged references.]


Citations from a Secondary Source[1]

McBride, Angela Barron. <u>A Married Feminist.</u> New York: Harper
    and Row, 1976.


[1]The bibliography entry is the source you used. The secondary source within
it will be shown in the documentation (see p. 121).

Privately Printed Book

Poetry in Crystal. New York: Steuben Glass, 1963.


## Periodicals

Magazine Article by Known Author, Successive Pagination in Volume

Polhemus, C. E. ''Due Process and Pregnancies.'' Monthly
    Labor Review, 99 (January 1976), 64–65.


Magazine Article by Known Author, Pagination by Issue

McCarthy, A. ''Displaced Homemaker.'' Commonweal, 16 January
    1976, pp. 38–40.

If periodical has volume number and/or individual issue number:

Cross, Patricia. ''The New Learners.'' Change, 5, No. 1
    (1973), 33–35.

[Omit abbreviation for pages when volume number is included.]


Scientific Magazine Article

Yao, S. C. and V. E. Schrock. Heat and mass transfer from
    freely falling drops. Journal of Heat Transfer. 98:
    120–26 (February 1976).

[Title does not need to be in quotation marks; each word does not
need to be capitalized; periodical title does not need to be underlined. Both volume and page numbers are given; date may be abbreviated.]


Magazine Article, Author Unknown

''How Women Feel About Their Lives Today: Survey.'' McCalls,
    April 1976, pp. 87–94.

Book or Film Review in Magazine

```
Gornick, Vivian. ''Neither Forgotten nor Forgiven.'' Rev.
     of Scoundrel Time, by Lillian Hellman. Ms, August 1976,
     pp. 46-47.
```

or

```
Maslin, Janet. ''Wild Pitch.'' Rev. of The Bingo Long
     Traveling All-Stars and Motor Kings. Newsweek, 19 July
     1976, p. 77.
```

Newspaper Article, Author Known

```
Seigel, Max H. ''Judge Scores U.S. on Draft Evaders.'' New
     York Times, 17 July 1976, sec. 1, p. 1, col. 4.
```

Newspaper Article, Author Unknown

```
''Kenya Defense Aide Says Army Would Crush Uganda Invasion.''
     New York Times, 17 July 1976, p. 3, cols. 1, 2.
```

[Column and page may be shown by numbers separated by a colon as in 3:2.]

Newspaper Editorial, Author Unknown

```
''Clearing the Murk.'' Editorial. The Tampa Tribune, 20
     July 1976, sec. A, p. 6, cols. 1-2.
```

Magazine Format Included as Newspaper Supplement

```
Miller, Judith. ''Bargain with Terrorists?'' New York Times
     Magazine [New York Times], 18 July 1976, pp. 7, 38-40,
     42.
```

## Other Sources

Published Dissertation or Thesis

```
Josey, E. J. What Black Librarians Are Saying. Diss.
     Metuchen, N.J.: Scarecrow Press, 1972
```

Unpublished Thesis or Dissertation

Dynner, Audrey Joan. ''Resources for Writers.'' Diss. Union
    Graduate School 1976.


Mimeographed or Dittoed Report

Michaels, David. Instructions for Students in English 101.
    Mimeographed. Miami, Florida.


Pamphlet by Known Author

Miller, Gustave. Patent Information. Miami: Library
    Reference, 1975.


Pamphlet by Unknown Author

Police Guide on Organized Crime. Washington, D.C.: Govern-
    ment Printing Office, 1976.


Letter, Personal or Unpublished

Lee, Sharon. Letter to the author and in his possession.
    22 November 1976.


or


Nightingale, Florence. Letter to Sir Arthur Landow.
    3 February 1898. In possession of Sheffield [England]
    Historical Society.


Interview or Lecture

Matz, Judith D. Interview, North Beach. 4 August 1975.
    by Raymond Normans, WJDM-TV. North Beach, 4 August
    1975, 8 P.M.


or


Matz, Judith D. Interview, North Beach. 4 August 1975.

Radio or TV Program

Allen, Roy. ''You and the Law.'' Radio talk. WDC, Washington.
    17 October 1974, 2 P.M.

or

''School's Out!'' Narrated by Eugene Dee. WCKT-TV, Miami,
    Florida. 12 June 1976, 3 P.M.


Videotape

<u>Forests</u> <u>and</u> <u>Man.</u> 60 min., sound, color, ¾ in. Narrated by
    Bob Weaver. Miami-Dade Community College, 1972.

or

<u>Individual</u> <u>Involvement.</u> Directed by Fred Wardell. 60 min.,
    sound, color, ¾ in. Miami-Dade Community College, 1972.

[If name of director is important, show it. Distributor is named as
if it were publisher, even though material is not produced by distributor.]


Filmstrip

<u>Your</u> <u>Diabetic</u> <u>Diet.</u> Color, 16mm cart., with phonotape.
    Train-Aide Educational Systems, 1972.

Film ( or Motion Picture Loop)

Welles, Orson, dir. <u>Citizen</u> <u>Kane.</u> With Orson Welles, Joseph
    Cotten, Dorothy Comingore, Agnes Moorehead, Ruth
    Warrick, et al. R.K.O. Radio Pictures, 1941.

[Information such as film size—for example, 16mm or super-8—or
running time may be given in parentheses after date if deemed important.]

If author of screenplay is of major importance in the research, put
that name first and give director's name after title of film:

Mankiewicz, Herman J., and Orson Welles. <u>Citizen</u> <u>Kane.</u> Dir.
    Orson Welles. With Orson Welles, Joseph Cotten, and
    others. R.K.O. Radio, 1941.

[The distributor's customary name only is used here.]

Theatrical or Musical Performance

[The first name given is the one that the writer wants to emphasize: the performer, the author, the director, the conductor, or whomever.]

American Ballet Theatre. <u>The Sleeping Beauty.</u> The Met, New
York. 5 May 1977.

Sonny & Cher. Westchester Premier Theatre. Westchester,
New York. 22 July 1977.

O'Neill, Eugene. <u>Anna Christie.</u> Dir. José Quintero. With Liv
Ullmann. Imperial Theatre, New York. 24 April 1977.

Phonograph Record or Audiotape

[List first the most important information: name of performer, composer, speaker, and so on.]

<u>Climb Every Mountain.</u> Mormon Tabernacle Choir. Columbia,
M30647, 1971.

Franck, Cesar. Symphony in D Minor. Cond. Leonard Bernstein,
New York Philharmonic. Columbia, ML-5391, 1959.

[Titles of pieces of music identified by number, key, or form are neither underlined nor put in quotation marks.]

<u>U.S.A. 2000: Three Alternative Views.</u> Carl Rogers, Alan
Watts, and Herman Kahn. Forum of Human Potentiality and
Human Growth. Big Sur Recordings, M221-2 (3¾ ips, 7"
reel), 1968.

or

Rogers, Carl, Alan Watts, and Herman Kahn. <u>U.S.A. 2000:
Three Alternative Views.</u> Forum of Human Potentiality
and Human Growth. Big Sur Recordings, M221-2 (3¾ ips,
7" reel), 1968.

Personal Interview

Roberts, Jason. Personal interview. 23 May 1977.

or

Aldama, Ciro. Interview recorded on audio cassette. Key
Largo, Florida. 1 August 1976.

Government Publications

> U.S. Bureau of the Census. <u>Census of Housing: 1970.</u> Washington, D.C.: GPO, 1971.

> U.S. Commission on International Trade and Investment Policy. <u>U.S. International Economic Policy in an Interdependent World, July 1971.</u> 3 vols. Washington, D.C.: GPO, 1971.

> State of Florida. Department of Transportation. Division of Planning and Programming. <u>1975 Environmental Directory.</u> Tallahassee, 1975.

> U.S. Cong. House. Committee on the Judiciary. <u>Impeachment Inquiry. Hearings Before the Committee on the Judiciary.</u> 93rd Cong., 2nd sess. H. Res. 803. 43 vols. Washington, D.C.: GPO, 1974–75.

## Documentation

Every footnote, endnote, or in-text reference must appear in the bibliography, but not every bibliographic entry will be represented by a note—only specific material that needs to be credited. The main difference between a text documentation and a bibliography entry is that the former shows precisely *where* in a source information was obtained: the page, the act, the line. There is a slight difference in order and in form so that the accommodation can be made, and it is not even necessary to repeat all the information after the original reference is cited. (See pp. 118–120 for first and subsequent note forms.)

The complete first reference form is illustrated on the following pages in the Standard Forms for notes.

*Paragraph indention form* is used for all documentation; that is, the first line of each note is indented five spaces and succeeding lines follow the usual left-hand margin of the page. Double-space all lines.

## Standard Forms for Notes

### Books

Book by Single Author

> ¹Gail Sheehy, <u>Passages: Predictable Crises of Adult Life</u> (New York: Dutton, 1976), p. 261.

## Book by Two Authors

[2]Nancy Gager and Cathleen Schurr, <u>Sexual</u> <u>Assault:</u> <u>Con-</u><u>fronting</u> <u>Rape</u> <u>in</u> <u>America</u> (New York: Grosset and Dunlap, 1976), p. 21.

## Book by Three or More Authors

[3]Martin D. Robbins, William S. Dorn, and John E. Skelton, <u>Who</u> <u>Runs</u> <u>the</u> <u>Computer?</u> (Boulder, Col.: Westview Press, 1975), p. 91.

## Organization or Institution as Author

[4]Women in Transition, Inc., <u>A</u> <u>Feminist</u> <u>Handbook</u> <u>on</u> <u>Separation</u> <u>and</u> <u>Divorce</u> (New York: Scribner's, 1975), p. 38.

## Book in Collaboration

[5]R. B. Fuller in collaboration with E. J. Applewhite, <u>Synergetics:</u> <u>Explorations</u> <u>in</u> <u>the</u> <u>Geometry</u> <u>of</u> <u>Thinking</u> (New York: Macmillan, 1975), p. 732.

## Book in Which Illustrator Is Important

[6]Dom Lupo, illustrator, <u>A</u> <u>Natural</u> <u>Way</u> <u>to</u> <u>Golf</u> <u>Power,</u> text by Judy Rankin (New York: Harper and Row, 1976), p. 118.

## Book, No Author Given

[7]<u>The</u> <u>Complete</u> <u>Dog</u> <u>Book</u> (New York: Howell Book House, 1975), p. 165.

## Author's Name Absent from Book but Known from Some Other Source

[8][Eugene Dynner,] <u>Camera</u> <u>Techniques</u> (Miami: Travelogue Press, 1977), pp. 2–6 passim.

## Book, Pseudonymous Author: Real Name Supplied

[9]Mark Twain [Samuel Langhorn Clemens], The Adventures of Huckleberry Finn (Boston: Riverside, 1968), p. 19.

[This is an optional form; pseudonyms usually are used alone.]

## Book Condensation of Longer Work

[10]Thomas Thompson, Lost. Condensed from Lost (Pleasantville, N.Y.: The Readers Digest Association, 1975), p. 65.

## Book, Single Editor or Compiler of a Collection

[11]Eve Meriam, comp., Growing Up Female in America: Ten Lives (New York: Doubleday, 1971), p. 261.

## Book, Multiple Editors or Compilers

[12]Martha T. S. Mednick et al., eds., Women and Achievement: Social and Motivational Analyses (New York: Halsted Press, 1975), p. 254.

or

[12]Martha T. S. Mednick and others, eds., Women and Achievement: Social and Motivational Analyses (New York: Halsted Press, 1975), p. 254.

## Anthology with No Editor Given

[13]A Malamud Reader, introd. Philip Rahv (New York: Farrar, Straus, and Giroux, 1967), p. 389.

## Poem in Anthology

[14]Barbara Ferland, ''At the University,'' in Caribbean Voices, selected by John Figueroa (New York: Robert B. Luce Co., 1973), p. 90.

or

[14]Gwendolyn Brooks, ''Old Laughter,'' Take Hold (Nashville: Thomas Nelson, 1974).

## Chapter in a Book by Author of Whole

[15]Jean-Paul Sartre, ''People's Theater and Bourgeois Theater,'' in <u>Sartre on Theater</u> (New York: Pantheon, 1976), p. 45.

## Article, Chapter, Story, or Essay in a Collection (Not by Author)

[16]Pat King, ''A Strategy for Change,'' in <u>Affirmative Action for Women,</u> eds. D. Jongeward and D. Scott (Reading, Mass.: Addison-Wesley, 1974), p. 139.

## Book Edited by Other Than Author of Contents

[17]Selma Jeanne Cohen, <u>A Sampler of Women's Studies: Papers,</u> ed. Dorothy Gies McGuigan (Ann Arbor: University of Michigan, 1973), pp. 36–42.

## Work of Author Contained in Collected Works

[18]John Webster, <u>The Tragedy of the Duchess of Malfi,</u> Vol. II of <u>The Complete Works of John Webster,</u> ed. F. T. Lucas (London: Chatto and Windus, 1927), p. 79.

## Several-Volume Work under General Title, with Each Volume Having Separate Title

[19]W. K. C. Guthrie, <u>Plato: The Man and His Dialogues: Earlier Period,</u> Vol. IV of <u>A History of Greek Philosophy</u> (London: Cambridge University Press, 1975), p. 197.

## Book in Series Edited by Other Than Author

[20]Jurgen Kranz, ed., <u>Epidemics of Plant Diseases,</u> in Ecological Studies, eds. J. Jacobs et al. (New York: Springer-Verlag, 1974), p. 27.

## Introduction by Other Than Author

[21]James Hamilton, <u>The Power to Probe: A Study of Congressional Investigations,</u> introd. Sam J. Ervin, Jr. (New York: Random House, 1976), p. 196.

## Work in Several Volumes

[22]Frank N. Magill, ed., <u>Masterplots,</u> 11 vols. (Englewood Cliffs, N.J.: Prentice-Hall, 1976), p.73.

## Translated Book, Known Author

[23]Otto Rank, <u>The Don Juan Legend,</u> trans. David G. Winter (Princeton, N.J.: Princeton University Press, 1975), p. 137.

## Translated Book without Author Separate from Title

[24]<u>Hans Bellmer/Sarane Alexandrian,</u> trans. Jack Altman (New York: Rizzoli, 1972), p. 59.

## Edition of a Book

[25]William S. Hoar, <u>General and Comparative Physiology,</u> 2nd ed. (Englewood Cliffs, N.J.: Prentice-Hall, 1975), pp. 731–735.

## Editon of a Book (Revised and Enlarged)

[26]Mario Dal Fabbro, <u>How to Build Modern Furniture,</u> rev. and enl. ed. (New York: McGraw-Hill, 1976), p. 188.

## Signed Encyclopedia Article

[27]Sidney Spencer, ''Christian Mysticism,'' <u>Encyclopaedia Britannica,</u> 15th ed. (1974).

[Volume and page numbers may be omitted from alphabetically arranged references.]

Unsigned Encyclopedia Article

²⁸''Maple Sugar Industry,'' <u>Encyclopedia</u> <u>Americana,</u> 1975.

[Volume and page numbers may be omitted from alphabetically arranged references.]

Citations from a Secondary Source

²⁹Jessie Bernard, <u>The</u> <u>Future</u> <u>of</u> <u>Motherhood</u> (New York: Dial, 1974), p. 103; cited by Angela Barron McBride in <u>A</u> <u>Married</u> <u>Feminist</u> (New York: Harper and Row, 1976), p. 99.

Privately Printed Book

³⁰<u>Poetry</u> <u>in</u> <u>Crystal</u> (New York: Steuben Glass, 1963), p. 30.

## Periodicals

Magazine Article by Known Author, Successive Pagination in Volume

³¹C. E. Polhemus, ''Due Process and Pregnancies,'' <u>Monthly</u> <u>Labor</u> <u>Review,</u> 99 (January 1976), 64.

Magazine Article by Known Author, Pagination by Issue

³²A. McCarthy, ''Displaced Homemaker,'' <u>Commonweal,</u> 16 January 1976, p. 39.

If periodical has volume number and/or individual issue number:

³³Patricia Cross, ''The New Learners,'' <u>Change,</u> 5, No. 1 (1973), 33.

[Omit abbreviation for pages when volume number is included.]

Scientific Magazine Article

Footnotes are usually recorded in one of two ways: (1) by number in parentheses in text corresponding to number in bibliography or (2) by year of source after name of authority cited in text. (See also pp. 124–125.)

Magazine Article, Author Unknown

[34]''How Women Feel About Their Lives Today: Survey,'' McCalls, April 1976, p. 91.

Book or Film Review in Magazine

[35]Vivian Gornick, ''Neither Forgotten nor Forgiven,'' rev. of Scoundrel Time, by Lillian Hellman, Ms, August 1976, p. 47.

or

[36]Janet Maslin, ''Wild Pitch,'' rev. of The Bingo Long Traveling All-Stars and Motor Kings, Newsweek, 19 July 1976, p. 77.

Newspaper Article, Author Known

[37]Max H. Seigel, ''Judge Scores U.S. on Draft Evaders,'' New York Times, 17 July 1976, sec. 1, p. 1, col. 4.

Newspaper Article, Author Unknown

[38]''Kenya Defense Aide Says Army Would Crush Uganda Invasion,'' New York Times, 17 July 1976, p. 3, col. 2.

[Column and page may be shown by numbers separated by a colon as in 3:2.]

Newspaper Editorial, Author Unknown

[39]''Clearing the Murk,'' Editorial, The Tampa Tribune, 20 July 1976, sec. A, p. 6, cols. 1-2 [6:A1-2 is alternate form after date of publication.]

Magazine Format Included as Newspaper Supplement

[40]Judith Miller, ''Bargain with Terrorists?'' <u>New</u> <u>York</u> <u>Times</u> <u>Magazine</u> [<u>New</u> <u>York</u> <u>Times</u>], 18 July 1976, p. 39.

## Other Sources

Published Dissertation or Thesis

[41]E. J. Josey, <u>What</u> <u>Black</u> <u>Librarians</u> <u>Are</u> <u>Saying,</u> Diss. (Metuchen, N.J.: Scarecrow Press, 1972), p. 39.

Unpublished Dissertation or Thesis

[42]Audrey Joan Dynner, ''Resources for Writers,'' Diss. Union Graduate School 1976, p. 28.

Mimeographed or Dittoed Report

[43]David Michaels, <u>Instructions</u> <u>for</u> <u>Students</u> <u>in</u> <u>English</u> <u>101,</u> mimeographed (Miami, Florida), p. 3.

Pamphlet by Known Author

[44]Gustave Miller, <u>Patent</u> <u>Information</u> (Miami: Library Reference, 1975), p. 23.

Pamphlet by Unknown Author

[45]<u>Police</u> <u>Guide</u> <u>on</u> <u>Organized</u> <u>Crime</u> (Washington, D.C.: Government Printing Office, 1976), p. 41.

Letter, Personal or Unpublished

[46]Sharon Lee, letter to the author and in his possession, 22 November 1976.

or

[47]Florence Nightingale, Letter to Sir Arthur Landow, 3 February 1898, in possession of Sheffield [England] Historical Society.

## Interview or Lecture

[48]Judith D. Matz, ''Women in the News,'' television interview by Raymond Normans, WJDM-TV, North Beach, 4 August 1975, 8 P.M.

or

[49]Judith D. Matz, interview, North Beach, 4 August 1975.

## Radio or TV Program

[50]Roy Allen, ''You and the Law,'' radio talk, WDC, Washington, 17 October 1974, 2 P.M.

or

[51]''School's Out!'' narrated by Eugene Dee, WCKT-TV, Miami, Florida, 12 June 1976, 3 P.M.

## Videotape

[52]Forests and Man, 60 min., sound, color, ¾ in., narrated by Bob Weaver, Miami-Dade Community College, 1972.

or

[53]Individual Involvement, directed by Fred Wardell, 60 min., sound, color, ¾ in., Miami-Dade Community College, 1972.

[If name of director is important, show it. Distributor is named as if it were publisher, even though material is not produced by distributor.]

## Filmstrip

[54]Your Diabetic Diet, color, 16 mm cart., with phonotape, Train-Aide Educational Systems, 1972.

## Film (or Motion Picture Loop)

[55]Orson Welles, dir., <u>Citizen Kane,</u> with Orson Welles, Joseph Cotten, Dorothy Comingore, Agnes Moorehead, Ruth Warrick, et al., R.K.O. Radio Pictures, 1941.

[Information such as film size—for example, 16mm or super-8—or running time may be given in parentheses after date if deemed important.]

If author of screenplay is of major importance in the research, put that name first and give director's name after title of film:

[56]Herman J. Mankiewicz and Orson Welles, <u>Citizen Kane,</u> dir. Orson Welles, with Orson Welles, Joseph Cotten, and others, R.K.O. Radio, 1941.

[The distributor's customary name only is used here.]

## Theatrical or Musical Performance

[The first name given is the one that the writer wants to emphasize: the performer, the author, the director, the conductor, or whomever.]

[57]American Ballet Theatre, <u>The Sleeping Beauty,</u> The Met, New York, 5 May 1977.

[58]Sonny & Cher, Westchester Premier Theatre, Westchester, New York, 22 July 1977.

[59]Eugene O'Neill, <u>Anna Christie,</u> dir. José Quintero, with Liv Ullmann, Imperial Theater, New York, 24 April 1977.

## Phonograph Record or Audiotape

[List first the most important information: name of performer, composer, speaker, and so on.]

[60]<u>Climb Every Mountain,</u> Mormon Tabernacle Choir, Columbia, M30647, 1971, Band 3.

[61]Cesar Franck, Symphony in D Minor, cond. Leonard Bernstein, New York Philharmonic, Columbia, ML-5391, 1959.

[Titles of pieces of music identified by number, key, or form are neither underlined nor put in quotation marks.]

[62]U.S.A. 2000: Three Alternative Views, Carl Rogers, Alan Watts, and Herman Kahn, Forum of Human Potentiality and Human Growth, Big Sur Recordings, M221-2 (3¾ ips, 7" reel), 1968.

## Personal Interview

[63]Personal interview with Jason Roberts, 23 May 1977.

[64]Interview recorded on audio cassette with Ciro Aldama at Key Largo, Florida, 1 August 1976.

## Government Publications

[65]U.S. Bureau of the Census, Census of Housing: 1970 (Washington, D.C.: GPO, 1971), p. 25.

[66]U.S. Commission on International Trade and Investment Policy, U.S. International Economic Policy in an Interdependent World, July 1971 (Washington, D.C.: GPO, 1971) vol. 2, pp. 6-8.

[67]State of Florida, Department of Transportation, Division of Planning and Programming, 1975 Environmental Directory (Tallahassee, 1975), p. 124.

[68]U.S. Cong., House, Committee on the Judiciary, Impeachment Inquiry, Hearings Before the Committee on the Judiciary, 93rd Cong., 2nd sess., H. Res. 803 (Washington, D.C.: GPO, 1974), Book III, p. 61.

# C

## STUDENT RESEARCH PAPER

Roslyn: Evolution of a Literary Character


by

Judith Matz


English 102
Dr. I. S. Kaufman
Pripichuk Junior College
August 4, 1976

Roslyn: Evolution of a Literary Character


THESIS: Arthur Miller used elements of a sophisticated mistress
in one story and a childlike wife in another to develop the
appealing but not fully explained character of Roslyn Taber in
The Misfits.


   I. Roslyn is an eastern sophisticate in ''The Misfits''
      (1957).
      A. She enjoys new sights and experiences.
      B. She feels sorry for hurt animals.
  II. Roslyn is a charming though essentially childlike figure
      in ''Please Don't Kill Anything'' (1960).
      A. She is fascinated by any new experience.
      B. She cannot bear to see anything die.
      C. She is sufficiently strong-willed to ask something of
         the man.
 III. Roslyn becomes a major character in The Misfits (1961).
      A. She seems innocent and vulnerable.
      B. She has a horror of death, reflected in her concern for
         animals.
      C. She has the power to change people.
         1. Guido and Perce realize their sham.
         2. Gay finds his own strengths.

Roslyn: Evolution of a Literary Character


        Seldom do we have the chance to watch a dramatic character
develop throughout various works by the same author. It is,
therefore, a fascinating glimpse into the mind of playwright
Arthur Miller to follow the growth of Roslyn. She is first
apparent in the thoughts of the cowboys, Gay, Perce, and Guido
in ''The Misfits,'' but does not actually appear in the story.
Roslyn is unmistakable, however, in another short story,
''Please Don't Kill Anything,'' although she is not named but
referred to as ''the girl.'' Miller finally combined the two
characters for the Roslyn of The Misfits, which he called a
cinema-novel because it used the perspective of film and its
images, and was the basis of the screenplay he wrote for the
film of the same name.

        The original story, published in 1957, grew out of an
experience Miller had with three Nevada cowboys. Finding themselves displaced by mechanized society, they now employ an
airplane to help them flush wild horses out of the mountains.
Once these mustangs were sought for riding; now they are sold
for dog food. Although the men are uneasy about this turn their
jobs have taken, they continue because the work represents
freedom and manhood. When their foray nets just five horses,
including a mare and her colt, their joyful independence sours,
and they return to town with the horses, but are embarrassed
and frustrated.

        The Roslyn of this story is the mistress of one of the
cowboys, Gay, and is spoken of with reverence by each of the
three men. They admire her for her sophistication and knowledge,
and seem a bit surprised that she sees anything of interest in
them.

        Arthur Miller tells of the youngest cowboy, Perce, musing,

''He had been surprised that an educated eastern woman should have been so regular and humorous and interested in his opinions.''[1]

Gay, agreeing with Perce that Roslyn would have loved to have seen the antelope they spotted, thinks of her ''eastern surprise at everything they did and saw and said,''[2] thus giving us a glimpse of the wonder-filled Roslyn of the future work.

The strongest hint of the part that Roslyn will play in the lives of these men comes after the mustang round-up: ''Roslyn goin' to feel sorry for the colt . . . so might as well not mention it,''[3] Gay tells the others.

This fascination with living things and horror at their destruction is central to the characterization of the girl in the 1960 short story, ''Please Don't Kill Anything.'' In it, a man and his wife are walking along the beach when they come upon fishermen hauling in their catch. The woman goes to look in the nets ''with the swift surge of wonder that swept through her at any new sight.''[4] In this quest for new experiences, she reflects the Roslyn of the earlier story.

When she realizes she is looking at dying creatures, she is deeply disturbed, even though she knows their death will serve a purpose.

> She glanced up at her husband and said, ''Oh dear, they're going to be caught now.''
>
> He started to explain, but she quickly went on, ''I know it's all right as long as they're eaten. They're going to eat them, aren't they?''
>
> ''They'll sell them to the fish stores,'' he said softly, so the old man at the winch wouldn't hear. ''They'll feed people.''
>
> ''Yes,'' she said, like a child reassured. ''I'll watch it. I'm watching it,'' she almost announced to him. But in her something was holding its breath.[5]

The girl persuades her husband to toss back into the sea the
fish that escape the net so they will not die needlessly. To
humor her, he does so, and they walk on, their relationship
cemented by his compliance with her demand, in spite of his
embarrassment.

An unmistakably parallel scene occurs in the cinema-novel,
The Misfits, when Roslyn realizes, with horror, the fate of the
captured horses.

> ''You kill them?''
>
> ''No, no, we sell them to the dealer.''
>
> Roslyn, her voice small, incredulous, even as some-
> where in her this news does not come as a surprise: ''He
> kills them?''
>
> Gay, with complete neutrality, as a fact: ''They're
> what they call chicken-feed horses—turn them into dog
> food. You know—what you buy in the store for the dog
> or the cat?''
>
> She has begun to quiver. He goes to her and starts
> to take her hand kindly. ''I thought you knew that.
> Everybody . . .''
>
> She gently removes her hand from his, staring incom-
> prehensibly into his face, turns, and walks into the
> darkness.
>
> ''. . . knows that.''[6]

In the cinema-novel, published four years after the first
story, we see a fully developed Roslyn, a Roslyn upon whom the
entire action turns. The reverence for life she shares with the
girl in ''Please Don't Kill Anything'' becomes the force in her
personality that causes profound changes in the lives of the
cowboys, especially Gay. And there is another similarity between

the girl of the short story and Roslyn: ''. . . their tenacity.
Beneath their naivete and wonder, the two women exhibit a strong
will and determination. Each gets her way.''[7] The girl wheedles
her husband into saving the fish; Roslyn impels her lover to
release the painfully captured horses.

The novel The Misfits, and the film script drawn from it, is
an American myth. It is set in Reno, a town symbolic of the
dying of the West, and peopled by aimless, shattered souls.
They have no foundation, no anchor, and they take little joy in
their way of life. The story ''is like a city built on shifting
sand; through it a search is going on for something stable in
the face of change . . . for a way out of chaos.''[8]

When Roslyn appears, she seems to provide a path through the
formless day. She is described by Miller as ''a golden girl
. . . the total effect is windy . . . but, quick as she is, a
certain stilled inwardness lies coiled in her gaze.''[9] She has
come to Reno to obtain a divorce because, as she accuses her
husband, ''You aren't there, Raymond! . . . If I'm going to be
alone, I want to be alone by myself.''[10]

Shortly after her divorce, Roslyn meets the cowboy, Gay, and
through him, his friends Guido and Perce, and together the four
embark on an odyssey in search of gaiety and companionship. They
appear at first to be capable of little understanding. ''They
are scatterbrained, whimsical, lonely . . . they are amusing
people to be with, for a little while, anyhow. But they are
shallow and inconsequential. . . .''[11] Roslyn and Gay become
lovers, and she agrees to accompany him and his friends, both
of whom are also attracted to her, on a venture into the mountains to capture wild mustangs. Their relationship, the first
of real substance in both their lives, is severely endangered
when Roslyn makes that discovery that these free souls are
destroying the horses for the money they collect from pet food
packers. Their lives are revealed, by Roslyn's horror, as shams;
they are slaves to the same civilization they profess to hate.

In a rush of self-awareness and love for Roslyn, the young
wanderer, Perce, lets the horses go. Gay's reaction is to
recapture two of them, alone and without the mechanical devices
they first used. Then, in a gesture of self-determination, he
frees them. Vindicated in Roslyn's eyes, and now unafraid to
face himself and the meaning of his life, they agree to try for
a future together.

This sketch of the story cannot convey the impact of The
Misfits, which The Times of London (30 May 1961, p. 18) has
found to be concerned with utter despair: ''Despair that modern
life makes true virility—equated with the frontier values of
the man without ties who must be his own master and for whom
anything is better than wages—impossible. Despair that whatever
one's intentions life makes a mockery of them and soils everything.''[12] Roslyn provides the only relief from this hopelessness, by demonstrating that the men can control their lives.

Echoing the bleak message, another critic finds:

> The Misfits is about death . . . on many levels: the
> death of a world—the West as it once was—and the death
> of a myth—the dream of the West as it never quite was;
> the death of human relationships and the destruction of
> personal values. On its most elemental level it is about
> the death of some misfit horses, which symbolize the
> figurative demise of some misfit people in a misfit
> world.[13]

What is Roslyn's part in all of this? In the beginning she
is like the men in her rootlessness and lack of purpose. Her
childlike innocence is the response of a woman who has never
fully matured. She has not allowed life to touch her because
she maintains her aloneness:

She walks unsteadily to the car, reaches in, and
pushes the switch. The lights go off. Now she stands
erect and looks up at the oblivious moon, a vast sadness
stretching her body, a woman whose life has forbidden
her to forsake her loneliness [my italics]. She cries
out, but softly, to the sky: ''Help!''[14]

In spite of her loneliness, or perhaps because of it, the
Roslyn of the novel has a great depth of feeling, as though she
has no barricade from the world around her. So she seems to be
totally vulnerable and identifies completely with hurt or
endangered animals—the horses, the rabbits that Gay wants to
shoot when they invade his garden, a frightened and whimpering
dog. While Miller makes Roslyn the embodiment of:

the lonely, the searching, and the lost . . . she is not
all waif. Roslyn is the most pitiful of fanatics. She is
gently drawn with an unmatched sensitivity; but together
with the knowledge that she is fragile goes an awareness that she is also resilient . . . her refusal to com-
promise is absolute . . . this is her strength.[15]

These characteristics are especially evident in her reaction to
Perce's injury while riding in a rodeo. She is bewildered by
the insensitivity of his friends, their acceptance of the
''macho'' creed, and at the same time is fiercely protective
and tries to physically restrain him from continuing in the
rodeo.

Indeed, her strength becomes the element of change, of a
move toward permanence, for all she comes in contact with. She

possesses this ''strength of character not immediately apparent behind her golden femininity, but crucial to her role in the lives of the misfits.''[16] For Roslyn provides the turning point in the piece, when she influences Gay to act out a change in his own carefully structured behavior. Her disgust, her outrage, leads to ''Gay's recapture of the mustang—nearly killing himself—and his symbolic freeing of it and, thereby, himself.''[17]

The two extremes of isolation represented by Roslyn and Gay move steadily towards each other, until they meet and make a commitment of sorts to each other. It is the first commitment with a chance of lasting for each of them, bruised as each is by former failures in their human relationships.

Roslyn learns at the end of the cinema-novel that violence and love are not mutually exclusive—they are both part of the human condition. When Gay acts with what she considers violence toward animals, this does not negate his capacity for love toward her. She learns not to categorize people. She also learns that ''a kind man can kill.''[18]

The book ends with Roslyn and Gay talking about a happy ending, looking for the way home. She says, ''How do you find your way back in the dark?'' (page 94), and he gives her a reassuring [but astronomically impossible] answer about heading for a certain star that is right over the highway. But we are given only a hint of what their eventual relationship might be.[19]

In spite of the fact that the Roslyn of all three literary works obviously has something that moves men profoundly, we never come to know just what, besides physical attractiveness, that something is. Much of what we know about her is not shown to us, but is told to us by the other characters when they talk to or about Roslyn. Critic Henry Popkin calls this, with sarcasm, ''characterization by compliment.''[20] That is, we know she is a wonderful human being because other people keep telling

her she is wonderful. For example, Guido says to her, ''When
you smile, it's like the sun coming up'' (The Misfits, p. 100).
And later in the novel, Gay tells her, ''I know you now, Roslyn.
I do know you. Maybe that's all the peace there is or can be
. . . it feels like I touched the whole world . . .'' (pp.
131–132). Guido also finds a whole world in Roslyn: ''. . . that
big connection. You're really hooked in; whatever happens to
anybody, it happens to you'' (p. 90).

At least one critic complains that we are justified in
expecting Roslyn to clarify the meaning of the ''gift of life''
that makes her a ''real woman.'' She frequently says things
about nature and animals that have a fresh, childlike imagery,
as when she wonders why birds are unafraid of flying in such a
huge sky. ''On the subject of human life, however, her youthful
wonderment changes to adolescent precocity . . . even her
hysterical denunciation of Gay's he-manship, perhaps her most
credible act, abounds in vague generalizations: 'Big man! You're
only living when you can watch something die! . . . You know
everything except what it feels like to be alive' (p. 118).
Again she leaves the point unclear.''[21]

Whatever the secret element in Roslyn, it serves to bring
about willing obedience in men. It would be too simple to say
that men want to win her approval, and so will risk acting in
ways that go against their impulses. The husband in ''Please
Don't Kill Anything'' and Gay in The Misfits are alike in this
willingness. But the differences in what the men are called
upon to do is great. Sam merely humors his wife; he makes a
game out of throwing the dying fish back into the water. But
the aging cowboy is responsible for the imminent death of the
horses, and he must redeem the animals in order to redeem
himself in Roslyn's eyes. His actions are a final statement of
the decision to change his whole way of life, and only Roslyn
has been able to cause his action, as well as have a place in
his new life.

We have seen the Roslyn of the original story, whom the men wanted too much to please, become the charming but somewhat cloying girl of a later Miller story. When she was transformed into a major character in The Misfits, Roslyn grew in complexity and lost the simple definition of innocence or sophistication that each of her ''ancestors'' had. In these three works Miller has provided us with an excellent view of the development of a dramatic character, from first sketches to boldly colored completeness.

Notes

[1]Arthur Miller, ''The Misfits,'' in I Don't Need You Any More (New York: Viking, 1967), p. 81.

[2]Page 90.

[3]Page 110.

[4]Arthur Miller, ''Please Don't Kill Anything,'' in I Don't Need You Any More (New York: Viking, 1967), p. 71.

[5]Page 72.

[6]Arthur Miller, The Misfits (New York: Viking, 1961), pp. 91–92.

[7]Benjamin Nelson, Arthur Miller, Portrait of a Playwright (New York: David McKay, 1970), p. 228.

[8]Sheila Huftel, Arthur Miller: The Burning Glass (New York: Citadel, 1965), p. 165.

[9]Misfits, p. 7.

[10]Misfits, p. 11.

[11]Bosley Crowther, ''The Misfits Reviewed,'' New York Times, 2 February 1961, p. 24, col. 2. The characters in the film are those of the cinema-novel.

[12]Quoted in Huftel, pp. 166–167.

[13]Nelson, p. 227.

[14]Miller, Misfits, pp. 87–88.

[15]Huftel, pp. 170–171.

[16]Nelson, p. 228.

[17]Eric Mottram, ''Arthur Miller: The Development of a Political Dramatist in America,'' in Arthur Miller: A Collection of Essays, ed. Robert W. Corrigan (Englewood Cliffs, N.J.: Prentice-Hall, 1969).

[18]Miller, Misfits, p. 94.

[19]Robert Corrigan, ed. Arthur Miller: A Collection of Essays (Englewood Cliffs, N.J.: Prentice-Hall, 1969), p. 12.

[20]''Arthur Miller Out West,'' Commentary, 31 May 1961, p. 435.

[21]Leonard Moss, Arthur Miller (New York: Twayne, 1967), p. 77.

## Bibliography

Corrigan, Robert W., ed. Arthur Miller: A Collection of Essays.
    Englewood Cliffs, N.J.: Prentice-Hall, 1969.

Crowther, Bosley. ''The Misfits Reviewed.'' New York Times,
    2 February 1961, 24:2.

Hogan, Robert. Arthur Miller. Minneapolis: University of
    Minnesota Press, 1964.

Huftel, Sheila. Arthur Miller: The Burning Glass. New York:
    Citadel, 1965.

Miller, Arthur. I Don't Need You Any More. New York: Viking,
    1967.

———. The Misfits. New York: Viking, 1961.

Moss, Leonard. Arthur Miller. New York: Twayne, 1967.

Nelson, Benjamin. Arthur Miller: Portrait of a Playwright. New
    York: David McKay. 1970.

Popkin, Henry. ''Arthur Miller Out West.'' Commentary, 31 (May
    1961), 433—436.

# Index

Abbreviations
  in card catalog, 44
  of commonly used terms, 74–75
Abstract, 133
Accuracy
  in notes, 69–72
  in writing, 104–105
Acknowledgments
  of direct play quotations, 110
  of direct poetry quotations, 109–110
  of direct prose quotations, 107–110
  forms of, 118–125, 158–168
  of ideas, 107, 112
  location of, 113–116, 117–118
  of maps, charts, diagrams, pictures,
    107, 112
  numbering system, 117–118
  of sources, 7, 9, 26, 107
Annotation
  on bibliography cards, 55
  defined, 132
  examples of, 132–133
Appendix, 133
Approaches to topics
  arguing, 38
  comparing and contrasting, 37
  examining, 36–37
  relating, 37–38
Approach, finding an, 35–38
Argument as an approach, 38
Assigned topics, 11–12
Audio-visual materials
  bibliography forms for, 156–158
  documentation forms for, 165–167
  as sources of information, 51, 52
Author card, 42

Background as opening, 96
Bad endings, 102–103
Bad openings, 97
Beginning of papers, 93–97
Bible, form for reference to, 123–124
Bibliography
  contents of, 130
  conventions of, 146–147

Bibliography (continued)
  defined, 130, 147
  form of, 130–131
  indexes, 49
  preliminary, 53–57
  types of, 131
Bibliography cards
  for books, 55, 56, 147–148
  contents of, 55, 56
  for encyclopedias, 57
  evaluating, 76
  for periodicals, 55, 56, 148
Body of paper, 97–100
Booklets, as sources of information, 52
Book references
  bibliography form for, 131, 148–153
  documentation form for, 118–120,
    158–163
Book review
  bibliography form for, 154
  documentation form for, 164
Books, publication information about,
  147
Borrowed ideas, acknowledging, 107
Brackets, square, 71

Card catalog, 41–46
  customs, 44–46
  order of entries, 45–46
  as source of ideas, 16
Casebooks, documentation of, 121–122
Catalog systems
  Dewey Decimal, 23–26
  Library of Congress, 23, 24
Cause to effect, organization by, 83–84
Challenging assumption as opening,
  94–95
Choosing a topic. See Topics
Clarifying topic as opening, 93
Combination notes, 64–65
"Common knowledge," 72, 107
Comparing and contrasting
  as approach, 37
  as organization, 82
Controlling idea, 78

Controversial topics, 28
Copying, without acknowledgment,
    9, 26, 107
Critical thinking, 10


Dewey Decimal Classification, 23, 25
Dictionary catalog, 41
Dissertations
    bibliography form for, 154–155
    documentation form for, 165
Divided catalog, 41–42
Documentation
    of Bible, 123–124
    content of, 116
    endnotes, 113–114
    footnotes, 114
    forms of, 107–125, 158–168
    interlinear, 114–115
    location of, 108–113
    nonprint media, 124, 165–167
    numbering system, 117–118
    of plays, 110
    of poetry, 109–110
    of prose, 108–109
    special problems of, 121–125
    in text, 115–116


Effect to cause, organization by, 83–84
Ellipsis, 71
Emphasis in paper, 78
Encyclopedia
    bibliography form for, 57, 152
    in choosing a topic, 13–16
    documentation form for, 162–163
    as source of research ideas, 13–16
Ending paper, 100–103
Endnotes, 114
Evaluation information, 6, 58–60,
    76–77
Examining as an approach, 36–37


Field-of-study topics, aids to choosing
    avocation, 19
    card catalog, 16
    defined, 12
    encyclopedia, 13–16
    personal interest, 19–21
    textbook, 13
    vocation, 21
Filing system, card catalog, 41–46

Film review
    bibliography form for, 154
    documentation form for, 164
First references, form of, 118–119
Five Ws, 33–34
Focal point, selecting, 31–34
Footnotes, location of, 114
Foreign prefixes in card catalog filing,
    44
Free association, 32
Free-choice topics, 22–26


General to particular, organization by,
    83
Good writing, 98–100
Government publications
    bibliography forms for, 158
    documentation forms for, 168


Hanging indentation form, 130, 148


Ibid., use of, 120
Illustrative material, 130
Information
    collecting, 5, 39–57
    recording, 58–75
Interlibrary loan, 51
Interlinear notes, 114–115
Interviews
    bibliography form for, 155, 157
    documentation form for, 166, 168
    as research source, 52
In-text documentation, 115–116
Investigative report, 4
Italics, 71, 129


Key words, 73
Known to unknown, organization by,
    82


Legibility of notes, 67–69
Length of paper, 4, 29, 54
Letters
    bibliography form for, 155
    documentation form for, 165
    as information source, 52
Library of Congress classification,
    23, 24

Library report, 4
Linking as ending, 102

Magazine indexes, 46–48
Materials, as criteria to determine
    length, 30
Mechanics in writing, 104
Methods of writing, 92–93
Microfiche, 51
Microfilm, 5

Names in card catalog, 42, 44
Narrowing topics, 29–38
Natural sciences documentation
    forms, 124–125
"Neutral" subjects, 28
Newspaper indexes, 48
Nonprint media
    bibliography forms for, 148, 156–157
    documentation forms for,
        124, 165–168
Note cards
    abbreviations on, 69, 75
    accuracy on, 69–72
    completeness, 72–73
    content, 61–73
    conventions of, 70–71
    evaluation of, 77–78
    form, 61–66
    identification on, 63, 65, 73
    legibility of, 67–69
    number of, 74
Notes
    combination, 64–65
    documentation, 129
    evaluation of, 77–78
    paraphrase, 63–64
    personal ideas, 65
    quotation, 61
    summary, 62–63
    types of, 60–67
Note taking
    general information, 60–73
    poetry, 71
    quotation acknowledgment, 70
    quotation within quotation, 71

Openings of research paper, 93–97
Order of material, 78

Organization
    of content, 81–84
    of ideas, 6, 76–91
    methods of, 81–84
Original work, 7
Outline
    content of, 87–90
    divisions of, 85
    explained, 84–91
    form for, 85–87
    indentation, 86
    information in, 87–88
    order of importance in, 89
    parallel phrasing, 90
    in presentation, 128–129
    punctuation in, 86
    reason for, 84
    relationship of ideas, 85, 86
    relation to thesis statement, 88
    revising, 90–91
    spacing, 87
    subordination in, 88
    symbols used, 85–86
    types of, 85
    typing, 129
Overworked topics, 28

Pamphlets
    bibliography form for, 155
    documentation form for, 165
    as source of information, 52
Paradox as opening, 95
Paragraph indentation form for
    documentation, 158
Paraphrase notes, 63–64
Particular to general, organization by,
    83
Periodical articles
    bibliography forms for, 131, 153–154
    documentation forms for, 119, 120,
        163–164
    publication information about, 49,
        148
Periodical indexes
    for choosing a topic, 16, 18
    as sources of information, 46–49
    use of, 49
Personal opinion, 9, 65
Photocopying, 73–74
Plagiarism, 9, 16, 107
    avoiding, 67
    unconscious, 66

Plays, form of documentation, 123
Poetry, forms in notes, 71
Preface of paper, 133
Preliminary bibliography
  defined, 53
  reasons for, 53
  uses of, 54
Presentation form
  abstract, 133
  annotations, 132–133
  appendix, 134
  bibliography, 130–131
  documentation, 129
  general information, 126–133
  illustrations, 130
  outline, 128–129
  preface, 133
  synopsis, 133
  text, 127, 129
  title page, 128
  typing, 127
Primary sources
  defined, 39
  importance of, 39
  location of, 39
Printed catalog, 42
Problem to solution, organization by,
  81, 83
Proofreading, 127
Punctuation
  for quotations, 61
  for quotations within quotations, 71

Qualities of writing, 98–100, 105
Question to answer, organization by,
  83
Questionnaires, 52
Quotations
  acknowledging, 70, 107–108
  do not constitute research paper, 8
  of drama, 110
  as ending, 101
  as opening, 95–96
  of poetry, 71, 109–110
  of prose, 108–109
  punctuation of, 70, 71–72, 108–111
  within quotation, 61, 110–111

Radio programs
  bibliography form, 156
  documentation form, 166

Radio programs (continued)
  as source of information, 52
Readers, documentation of, 122–123
*Readers' Guide to Periodical
  Literature*, 16, 20, 46–47
Reference words and abbreviations,
  74–75
Reference works available in library,
  135–145
Relating
  as an approach, 37–38
  as an opening, 94
Reports, 4, 8
  as source of information, 52
Research
  applied, 3
  business, 4
  market, 4
  pure, 3
  scholarly, 3
  sources of information, 39–57
  technical, 4
Research paper
  basic technique of, 5–7, 9–10
  characteristics of, 77
  defined, 4, 7
  participant in, 4
  personal advantages of, 9–10
  sample student paper, 171–183
  writing, 92–106
Return to statement, as ending,
  101–102
Reusing papers, 26
Revising writing, 103–105

Scientific article
  bibliography, 125, 131
  documentation form, 124–125
Secondary sources
  defined, 39–40
  location of, 40
"See also" card, 18, 44
Selecting research topic, 11–28
Sentence outline, 85, 86, 90
Simple to complex, organization by, 82
Single source topics, 26
Slugs, 61–65, 73
Sourcebooks, documentation of,
  121–122
Source material
  availability, 30
  evaluating, 58–60

Source material (continued)
  in topic selection, 30
Sources of information, 39–57
Specialized library collections, 51
Square brackets, use of, 71
Stating position
  as ending, 100–101
  as opening, 93–94
Statistics as opening, 96
Student research paper, 171–183
Style of writing, 92–93
Subdividing, 31–32
Subject card, 43–44
Subjects. *See* Topics
Subject subdivisions in catalog, 45
Subsequent references, forms for,
  119–120
Summary
  is not a research paper, 8
  notes, 62–63
Supporting statement, 98
Synopsis, 133

Television programs
  bibliography form for, 156
  documention form for, 166
  as source of information, 52
Term paper, 4
Textbook, for topic ideas, 13
Thesis statement, 78–80
  defined, 78
  function of, 78–79
  not a question, 80
  not a title, 79–80
  not a topic, 79
Title card, 42–43
Title page, 128
Titles
  in card catalog, 42–44
  for research paper, 105–106
Topic
  assigned, 11–12
  field-of-study, 12–22
  free choice, 22–26

Topic (continued)
  outline, 85–90
  overused, 28
  unfruitful, 28
Topics
  to avoid, 26–28
  choosing, 5
  controversial, 28
  narrowing, 29–38
  neutral, 28
  overworked, 28
Transitions in writing, 99, 104
Typing
  of annotation, 133
  of documenting notes, 118, 127
  of outline, 87, 123
  of quotations, 108–110
  of research paper, 121, 133

*Vertical File Index*, 51

Writing
  accuracy, 104–105
  body of paper, 97–100
  clarity, 99
  coherence, 98–99
  conciseness, 100
  concreteness, 100
  consistency, 99
  documentation in, 117
  emphasis, 99
  endings, 100–103
  mechanics, 104
  methods of, 92
  openings, 93–97
  the paper, 6, 92–106
  proofreading, 127
  quality of, 105
  revision of, 103–105
  sentence structure, 104
  style, 92–93
  unity, 98
  word choice, 103